PENGUIN BOOKS
SUBHĀSHITĀVALI

Aditya Narayan Dhairyasheel Haksar was born in Gwalior and educated at the Doon School and the universities of Allahabad and Oxford. A well-known translator of Sanskrit classics, he has also had a distinguished career as a diplomat, serving as Indian high commissioner to Kenya and the Seychelles, minister to the United States, and ambassador to Portugal and Yugoslavia.

His translations from the Sanskrit include *Hitopadeśa* and *Simhāsana Dvātrimśikā*, both published as Penguin Classics, *Jatakamala* (with a foreword by the Dalai Lama) published by HarperCollins India, and the first-ever rendition of *Madhavanala Katha*, published by Roli Books as *Madhav and Kama*. He has also compiled *A Treasury of Sanskrit Poetry*, which was commissioned by the Indian Council for Cultural Relations.

SUBHĀSHITĀVALI

An Anthology of Comic, Erotic and Other Verse

Selected and translated from the Sanskrit

by

A.N.D. Haksar

PENGUIN BOOKS

PENGUIN BOOKS

Published by the Penguin Group

Penguin Books India Pvt. Ltd, 11 Community Centre, Panchsheel Park, New Delhi 110 017, India

Penguin Group (USA) Inc., 375 Hudson Street, New York, New York 10014, USA

Penguin Group (Canada), 90 Eglinton Avenue East, Suite 700, Toronto, Ontario, M4P 2Y3, Canada (a division of Pearson Penguin Canada Inc.)

Penguin Books Ltd, 80 Strand, London WC2R 0RL, England

Penguin Ireland, 25 St Stephen's Green, Dublin 2, Ireland (a division of Penguin Books Ltd)

Penguin Group (Australia), 250 Camberwell Road, Camberwell, Victoria 3124, Australia (a division of Pearson Australia Group Pty Ltd)

Penguin Group (NZ), cnr Airborne and Rosedale Roads, Albany, Auckland 1310, New Zealand (a division of Pearson New Zealand Ltd)

Penguin Group (South Africa) (Pty) Ltd, 24 Sturdee Avenue, Rosebank, Johannesburg 2196, South Africa

Penguin Books Ltd, Registered Offices: 80 Strand, London WC2R 0RL, England

First published by Penguin Books India 2007

Copyright © A.N.D. Haksar 2007

10 9 8 7 6 5 4 3 2 1

ISBN-13: 978-0-14310-136-9 ISBN-10: 0-14310-136-6

Typeset in Sabon by S.R. Enterprises, New Delhi
Printed at Sanat Printers, Haryana

P. M. S.

For Sharada, Vikram and Annika with love

Contents

Introduction	ix
Prologue	1
1. Salutations	2
2. Blessings	6
3. Poets and Poetry	11
4. Good People	15
5. Villains	20
6. Niggardliness	24
7. Nobility	26
8. Allegories from Nature	29
9. Allegories from the Animal World	36
10. Allegorical Miscellany	43
11. Love in Separation	46
12. Friends and Go-betweens	55
13. Beautiful Women	62
14. Pride and Placation	65
15. The Seasons	71
16. Nightfall	79
17. Carousals	84
18. Love in Union	87

19. Miscellaneous Verses: 1   97
20. The Heroic Mode   100
21. Humour and Satire   102
22. Pen Pictures   121
23. Verses of Flattery   124
24. Verses of Counsel   127
25. On Dharma   134
26. The Iron Age of Kali   138
27. The Power of Past Deeds   141
28. Fate   143
29. Times of Trouble   147
30. On Being a Servant   151
31. Cravings   153
32. Transience   156
33. Derision of Lust   161
34. Regrets   165
35. Aspiration   167
36. Miscellaneous Verses: 2   169
37. Prayers   174

The Poets   177
Notes   185

Introduction

The Sanskrit word *subhāshita* can be translated literally as 'well said'. It is often used for an epigrammatic stanza, the meaning or mood of which is complete in itself. Such a verse, also known as *muktaka*, could be an independent composition or part of a larger work. Its themes had a large variety, but its form was a constant two metric lines of equal weight, sometimes presented in four sections because of their length. At its best it combined brevity with a felicitous compression of thought or emotion. Many such verses passed into literature as maxims, proverbs or just memorable, quotable poetry.

Subhāshita verses are a characteristic and popular feature of classical Sanskrit literature. A recognized art form, they occur in the great epics, as a part of longer poems, and in plays and prose works. Much esteemed in cultured intercourse, they lent themselves to collection in anthologies. A number of these, compiled in various parts of the country during the last one thousand years, are extant.[1] Prominent among them is *Subhāshitāvali*, or a circlet of well-said verses, from which a selection is presented here in translation.

The contents of some *subhāshita* compilations are confined to a single theme or attributed to a single author.[2] Others bring together verses by numerous authors on a wide range of subjects.[3] *Subhāshitāvali* is of the second type. It is a collection of 3527 verse epigrams, grouped under 101 subject headings, and ascribed by name to 362 poets, apart from the many which are anonymous.

Academic opinion dates *Subhāshitāvali* to c. fifteenth century CE.[4] Its compiler was Vallabhadeva, who is described in some texts as a *kāshmīraka*, a person from Kashmir.[5] Little

else is known about him but the anthology's Kashmiri
connection is also evident from a number of authors and verses
that feature in it. The former are noted in the appended list of
poets and some of the verses, such as vv. 118, 243, 332 and
452, are included in the present selection. The subject of one
(v. 425) is clearly Sultan Zainu'l Abidin (1420–1470),[6] a
famous ruler of Kashmir who is known to have patronized
Sanskrit letters. Thus, apart from the literary wealth of its
contents, the compilation is also a pointer to the prevalence
and extent of Sanskrit learning in medieval Kashmir.

The *Subhāshitāvali* verses span a period of at least 1500 years
preceding the time of its compilation. Those extracted from
the epics—*Mahābhārata* and *Rāmāyana*—are probably much
older. The variety is immense. The anthology begins and ends
on a devout note of divine invocations. In between, there are
reflections on poets and poetry, on virtue and wickedness,
nobility and meanness. There are numerous allegorical
epigrams and verses on nature. Not unexpected, there is a
rich collection of erotic poetry on all aspects of love, symbolic
and actual, emotional as well as physical. This is followed by
heroic, humorous and satiric verses, panegyrics and pen-
pictures, and sage observations on worldly conduct. Finally
there are musings on the human condition, on its transience
and insignificance, and on moral duty and renunciation.

The tone of these epigrams ranges from the pious to the
profane, the lyrical to the sententious, the earnest to the
cynical, the elegant to the somewhat coarse. Some are drawn
from famous works; others are known only from their
presence in this collection. The authors, likewise, include
celebrated poets like Vālmiki and Vyāsa, Kālidāsa and Bāna,
as well as many who are no more than names.

In modern times, a manuscript of *Subhāshitāvali* was
located by the British scholar Peter Peterson with Pandit Durga
Prasad of Jaipur, who had studied it in Kashmir. Collating it

with other manuscripts from the same land and elsewhere, Peterson edited and published the anthology's Sanskrit text in 1886 at Mumbai. Still the only critical recension in existence, it was reprinted in 1961 by the Bhandarkar Oriental Research Institute of Pune, and forms the basis for the present translation.

Though reputed in academic circles, *Subhāshitāvali* is little known to general readership. According to available records, it has never been translated into English, except for a few stanzas from its corpus included in some histories of Sanskrit literature or in some selections of Sanskrit poetry.[7] Thus its treasure of epigrams remains largely inaccessible to modern readers. The present work attempts to ameliorate this situation by providing a representative sampling in contemporary English from the anthology's poetic cornucopia.

The selection presented here consists of 600 verses, or just under a fifth of the original. This size seemed optimal for publication, but some mention of the criteria of selection would still be appropriate. Within the limits of space, choice was based mainly on the consideration that translations of poetry should as far as possible be readable on their own, without requiring supplementary explanations about their intent and context. Thus, verses which rely for their impact on Sanskrit figures of speech and linguistic devices like paranomasia and alliteration, and others of the type *vakrokti* or oblique language, based on multiple meanings of words or suggestions, were largely left out.[8] So too were most verses with mythological or other esoteric allusions which may be unfamiliar to the general reader. Some incomplete or unclear verses in the text were also excluded.

As for the actual selection, the effort was to make it representative of the original anthology as a whole by drawing verses from all its subject headings. Quality, translatability and, in some cases, historical interest were other considerations in choosing individual stanzas for translation. Additional

attention was given to the *hāsya* section of the original, which
deals with humour and satire, as there are few English
translations of this genre of Sanskrit verse.

The verses selected have been grouped under thirty-seven
subject headings. Most of these correspond, in the same order,
to the individual headings from the original's *sūchipatra* or
table of contents, but there has been a measure of clubbing
together in two instances, which requires further elaboration.

The first is the original's section on *anyāpadeśa*, or the
allegorical epigram. The charactersitic of this composition,
to quote the American Sanskritist D.H.H. Ingalls, 'is that the
person or situation expressly described serves to suggest some
person or situation which is not mentioned, but to which the
moral or the point of the verse applies'.[9] For example, an
epigram about the lion (v. 120) suggests that true excellence
is innate and not dependent on any endorsement by others.
The anthology has twenty subject headings under this section,
describing specific animals and natural phenomena to suggest
human qualities and situations. These have been combined
here in three headings (8, 9 and 10) as allegories from nature,
the animal world and a miscellany.

The second is the anthology's section on *śringāra*, or the
erotic mode in its manifold aspects. The anthology has no
less than fifty-two subject headings under this section, here
combined into nine (11 to 19). The first of these (11) clubs
four original headings on the pangs of separation suffered by
lovers. The second (12) encompasses six from the original
list about the trials faced by separated lovers, the questions
and admonitions of friends, and the need to resort to messengers,
often a girl who may well try to supplant the beloved in the
lover's attentions.

The third heading (13) in the present selection combines
eighteen from the original, including sixteen on the anatomy
of feminine beauty. It was conventional to describe this in
minute detail with traditional comparisons and the anthology
has separate headings for various parts of the female body,

from the forehead to the feet, and much that lies in between. These have been put together to present an overall picture without excessive and repetitive attention to minutiae.

The next combination (14) is of three original headings about the woman in love feeling offended, the placatory efforts of her lover and their exchanges. Following it, six original headings on the seasons are clubbed under one (15), and three on trysts at night under another single heading (16). The final combination (18) brings together seven original headings, from the exchange of endearments to the commencement, the climax and the end of love-making, with the verses selected ranging over the full erotic cycle. It is followed by a miscellany (19), the second of the three which are included in the original anthology.

The number of epigrams under humour and satire (21) is marginally the largest of all in this selection. The reason, as already mentioned, is that such verses have been little translated and remain comparatively unknown. Sanskrit literature, with the overall scholarly emphasis on its religious and philosophical content, is generally perceived as staid and serious. Its lighter, more flippant side has normally been overshadowed by great and solemn works. Here this side can be glimpsed in stanzas of jollity and wit, ribaldry and satire, harsh sarcasm and earthy bawdiness. Without condoning the sexism reflected in some of them, such verses have been included to enable *subhāshita* poetry to be seen in its totality.

The other subject headings of this selection need little comment. Each has a separate counterpart in the same order in the original, and most are self-explanatory. The word *dharma* (25), left as in the original, has multiple meanings, but its sense here is mainly moral duty and virtuous conduct. The word *Kali* (26) refers to the present age in Indian mythology, which is a time of extreme degeneration in contrast to the ages which preceded it. The next heading (27) which reads *karma* in the original draws on the concept that the present condition of all beings is determined by their past deeds.

My translations have endeavoured to combine fidelity to the original verses with the requirements of modern English usage. If some are longer than the others it is because this was necessary for giving due expression to the ideas or images compressed in individual stanzas. Inflection, compounding and syntax in Sanskrit give greater scope for such compression than is possible in English, and the two or four lines of an original stanza sometime needed up to twelve in English to fully convey its meaning and intent. I have also used a variety of verse forms to reflect as far as possible some of the colour and flavour of the originals instead of literal renditions in prose.

The ascription of the verses presented here has been shown exactly as it occurs in the original. In many cases there is none. In others authors are named with or without titles or in both forms, for example Valmiki and Valmiki Muni. In a few cases the reference is to a work and not an author. Present scholarship shows that some of the compiler's ascriptions, perhaps based on the information available to him at the time, are not correct. These have been pointed out as far as possible in the notes. Seventeen verses in the original bear the name Vallabhadeva, but it is difficult to say with certainty which of them are by the compiler and which by an earlier writer with the same name from c. tenth-century Kashmir. Peterson assigned the two stanzas in the anthology's prologue (vv. 1 and 2) to the compiler, though his edited text gives them as anonymous.

Standard diacritics have been used in spelling the names of poets and the titles of texts, but otherwise confined largely to the indication of long vowels. Names in common usage, like Krishna and Shiva, have been spelt in this form which is easier to read. A brief background to the gods and goddesses mentioned in the verses is given at the beginning of the notes. Individual notes give information on specific verses, mainly their sources where known. The serial number of each verse, as given in the original anthology, has been shown at its right to facilitate reference to the Sanskrit text.

In preparing the notes and the details of the poets, I have relied mainly on Peterson's erudite annotations and some information on writers derived from D.D. Kosambi's introduction to the Sanskrit text of another anthology.[10] I also benefited from consulting R. Malaviya's edition of the Peterson text (Varanasi, 1974) with notes and translations in Hindi, though his identification of our compiler with his tenth-century namesake needs further research for a definite conclusion.

Like any good anthology of poetry, *Subhāshitāvali* contains verses for all tastes and occasions. Some are of the highest quality, others may seem pedestrian by modern reckoning, but all are epigrammatic, clipped and to the point. It is not difficult to imagine that they were compiled to be read for pleasure and to be used for reference or quotation on appropriate occasions. I have enjoyed reading Vallabhadeva's original collection over the years, and am glad to share it with others through this translation.

I am grateful to V.K. Karthika, executive editor, Penguin India, for her ready response which encouraged me to undertake the present work. Some sample translations were seen earlier by my friends Ranjit Mathur and the late Ravi Dayal to whom I am indebted for the trouble they took to comment on them. Thanks are also due to Jaishree Ram Mohan for her meticulous copy-editing of my typescript. But most of all I would like to thank my wife, Priti, who read through most of the drafts and redrafts with enormous patience and always helpful criticism. For all her support in this and many other ways, no words of my gratitude can ever be adequate. Nor can they be for my mother, Subhadra, my first mentor in Sanskrit, whose birthday is today.

A.N.D.H.

Noida
5 September 2006

Prologue

1

All praise to Sharada,
the goddess enthroned
on white autumnal clouds,
adept dispeller
of the pain existence
brings in its wake.   1

2

Hail to the power
of human thought,
which needs no word
of any guru
to pierce through all
the veils, revealing
secrets supreme.   2

1. Salutations

3

I bow to that radiance,
peaceful and still,
endless, unbound
by space and time,
which is the spirit,
and only known
through self-awareness.   3

BHARTRIHARI

4

Reverence to Brahma,
a flutter of whose eyes
is sufficient cause
for the world's creation
and its dissolution.   4

PRAKĀŚAVARSHA

5

Bow to Vishnu,
the cause original
of the world's creation,
its being and end.
He is the bridge
across this endless
course of life and death.   5

PUNYA

6

Bow to the great boar
who saved the earth
with playful ease:
the mountain Meru
is but a speck
beneath his hooves.   7

7

Bow to Shambhu,
his head caressed
by the crescent moon;
he is the rock
on which are built
the mansions of
the triple world.   8

BHAṬṬA BĀṆA

8

Even the gods pray to him
for realization of their wishes:
reverence to that Ganapati,
remover of all obstacles.   9

9

Homage to Manmatha,
churner of the mind,
who dwells in lovely women
with round, uplifted bosoms,
comely hips and languid gait.   10

VIṬA VRITTA

10

Homage to that light supreme
which seems diverse
in different forms
but in essence is the same,
like gold in varied ornaments
and water in lake or sea.

14

11

Whichever the worship
it is of him;
wherever the prayer,
it is to him;
whatever the form,
this or another,
it is but his.
Homage to him, to God.

19

12

Reverence to Shambhu,
who transcends
the double state
of is and is not
into a wondrous third.

20

13

Bow to him who is the word
both occult and manifest,
his glory revealed by the power
of the independent mind.

21

14

Homage to Shambhu,
the wondrous and marvellous;
he is near, yet so far,
both easy and difficult to reach,
hidden, and yet so manifest.   22

15

Be it Vishnu or Shiva,
Brahma or the king of gods,
the sun, the moon, or the Buddha,
or some other perfect being:
salute the one
devoid of the poison
of likes and dislikes
with their pain and delusion,
adorned with every merit,
and compassionate to all.   24

16

This verse by Svami Datta,
the poet whose name marks the work
called *Chakrapāni Jaya,*
is here included
in his memory.   25

17

On his brow a dot of musk,
on his breast the sacred jewel,
a fresh new pearl upon his nose ring,
a string of gems around his throat,
his limbs adorned with sandal paste,
the flute within his gleaming hands,
ringed by milkmaids: glory be
to the prince of cowherds, and victory.   27

2. Blessings

18

May Vishnu's arms protect you,
strong as tree trunks,
dark as clouds,
givers of bounty,
reflecting the trace
of a leaf design
on Lakshmi's cheek.   29

HARSHADATTA

19

May the great boar's mighty tusk,
which holds the earth as in a swing,
pales the glow of the crescent moon,
and lights the depths of the nether world,
protect and guard you all.   30

MĀTANGA DIVĀKARA

20

When Hari held up
the hill Govardhana,
all the cowherds
were overjoyed.
Listening to their
songs of praise,
he remembered
his form as a boar,
with the earth uplifted
on the crescent
of his tusk,
and smiled, embarrassed.
May that shy smile
guard you all.   34

                                        VIBHŪTIBALA

21

May that wind protect you all—
the breath of god in tortoise form,
as he slept, his back caressed
by the whirling peak of Mount Mandara
which churned the sea in times gone by.
That breathing caused a tide to rise,
and even now the ebb and flow
of oceans does not ever cease.   36

22

May Krishna's smile protect you all
as, eyes half shut, he drinks his fill
from one breast, then grasps the other
on which a drop has just appeared;
he beams as his chin is tickled,
his little teeth gleaming
like tiny drops of milk.   37

23

'While your brother's gone to play
on the Yamuna's sandy banks,
Hari quickly drink your milk—
it is from the brindled cow
and will make your hair grow long.'
The child, thus cozened by Yashoda,
drinks half the milk, then stops to feel
the hair upon his head, and beams.
May that Hari guard you all.   38

JĪVAKA

24

Yashoda looks at him with joy;
the milkmaids long and ardently;
with smiles the gods, respect, the sages;
young men with envy; kindly, the old;
his foes are fearful of his power,
and the earth besides itself,
as Krishna lifts the hill Govardhana:
may he protect you all.   39

BHAṬṬA CHÚLITAKA

25

'Mother, Krishna goes to play
and swallows mud deliberately.'
'Krishna, is this true?' 'Says who?'
'Your brother.' 'Mama, it's a lie,
look at my mouth.' 'Then open it.'
And within the mouth, a marvel,
the mother sees the world entire!
May that Krishna guard you all.   40

CHANDAKA

26

'I stay devoted by your side
and think of no one else.
Is it proper that you leave me
and sport with all these mistresses?'
Waking Hari with these words,
then finding that the myriad images
in the serpent's jewelled hoods
are but her own reflections,
Lakshmi smiles abashed.
May her smile protect you all.   41

27

They shame blue lotuses,
look lovingly at devotees,
are the focus of meditation
for sages seeking merit.
They are a mine of beauty
and gladden Lakshmi's heart:
may Hari's eyes and person rid you
of sufferings in this scheme terrestrial.   43

AMRITADATTA

28

May Hari's conch shell bless you all,
the sound of which, when it is blown,
rends enemy hearts, surpassing the roar
of the seven seas churning within his belly.   47

29

In the van of battle, when
Hari gazes at his discus,
searing flames arise from it
and spread in all directions,
a blazing image of the sun
which is but his eye.
May that discus now dispel
the circle of your enemies.   49

ANANDAVARDHANA

30

'Mother!' 'Darling!' 'What is hidden
in father's hands he clasps together?'
'A tasty fruit, my child.' 'But why
then does he not give it to me?'
'Go and take it yourself!'
By his mother thus set up,
when Guha pulled the hands apart
and disturbed his meditation,
Shambhu curbed his anger and
burst out laughing.
May that laughter
protect and guard you all.   69

CHANDAKA

3. Poets and Poetry

31

What is the worth
of the poet's verse,
or the archer's dart,
which cannot set
the mind awhirl
as it strikes the heart?   134

32

What is the use
of a poem's nectar,
drenched by whose
sweet flow of feeling
the mind obtuse
can still not bloom?   136

ŚRI KALLAṬA

33

Some villains with no intellect
to compose even two lines
are ever ready to criticize
the hard work of other poets.   140

BODHAKA

34

'What fault can I find?'
With this thought in mind
does a villain always start
to scrutinize a poet's art.   141

BHAṬṬA NĀRĀYAṆA

35

Some parrot poetry;
others have it inside
but are struck dumb;
rare is someone
from whose heart, bubbling,
flow graceful verses
straight to the tongue.   143

ARCHITADEVA

36

The language of a master poet,
the pledge of wholesome speech observing,
is splendid like a woman chaste,
untouched by vulgar word or meaning.   145

PRABHĀKARANANDA

37

Those great souls we should revere,
their fame will last eternally,
who have created poems, or
whose praise is sung in poetry.   146

38

Even verses void of elegance,
but timely read, are brilliant thought;
just as tasteless food is savoured
by one with hunger overwrought.   150

VALLABHADEVA

39

The lotus grows in water
but blossoms with the sun;
the poet simply writes the poem,
good people make it known.   154

BHADANTA RAVIGUPTA

40

With a verse stuck in his throat,
the poet suffers as it were
the last gasp of his very life
till his eyes alight upon
someone with understanding.   156

AMRITADATTA

41

The language of great poets has
yet another, inner, sense,
like a woman's grace, which is
from her limbs a thing apart.   157

ANANDAVARDHANA

42

The poet's unsaid thought will only
throb within some tender verse:
my homage to one who is silent,
but responds with a thrill.   158

VIJJĀKĀ

43

Patronage of poets brings
kudos and repute to kings,
for poets the very same
opens many doors to fame.
There is no patron better than
a king for men of poetry,
for kings too, there never can
a helper like a poet be.   160

BHAṬṬA GOVINDASWAMI

44

Śri Harsha gave a hundred measures
of gold to Bāna, worthy poet,
and a herd of rutting elephants too.
Where is all that wealth today?
But the multitude of verses
that Bāna coined in Harsha's praise
will, I hold, remain unblemished
till the very end of time.   180

45

King Rama was extolled by Valmiki;
Dharma's son by Vyasa;
Śri Vikrama, lord of men,
by Kalidasa the poet;
Bhoja by Chittapa and Bilhana;
and Karna by Vidyapati.
These monarchs became famous
because of great poets,
not by the tumult
of their battle drums.   186

4. Good People

46

As clusters of wild flowers do,
the high-minded have but courses two:
to be borne on every brow,
or perish on some forest bough.   201

RAVIGUPTA

47

For even those devoid of merit
the good always compassion bear:
the moon does not its lustre limit
in lighting up the outcaste's lair.   225

48

The base will sin because they're cruel;
when terror strikes, so may the weak;
but the good, their lives at peril,
can no more sin than can the sea
roll o'er its natural boundary.   272

BHADANTA ŚŪRA

49

Can any burden be too great
for those of fit and able state?
What destination is too far
for those who enterprising are?
Which country is a foreign land
for those with knowledge? And
who can be the enemy
of those who will speak lovingly?   313

50

They cannot stand to be obliged
and will not tolerate sympathy,
the high-minded are hard to help—
they can never happy be.   202

51

The rising sun is red,
and also red at setting.
The great will look the same
in good times and in bad.   220

52

Courage in calamity,
forgiveness in victory,
in warfare chivalry,
eloquence in assembly,
love of reputation,
to scriptures devotion:
this is the true nature
of men of noble stature.   267

53

Men of merit lasting long
is intolerable even to fate:
the moon stays only for one night
in its full and glorious state.   301

54

Experts may deride them
or praise them to the sky,
glory may crown them
or just pass them by,
death may be an age in coming
or strike this very day:
the good will not hesitate from stepping
on the righteous way.   278

55

The well-bred, even though enraged,
will never scurrilous language use;
when pressed, the sugar cane exudes
only sweetness in its juice.
The base, however, even served
with every kind of skill,
can in jest say things which hurt,
cause quarrels and ill will.   277

56

One who has bathed
in the cool, bright stream
of good people's company:
what does he need
of pilgrimage and penance,
of rites and ceremony?   211

VALMIKI MUNI

57

The good do not give up their nature,
struck even by calamity:
camphor, burning in the fire,
will never fragrant cease to be.   296

58

What is so special
in kindness to one
who has done you a favour
or bears no ill will?
But one who has harmed you,
now caught for the crime:
the mind which is moved
by compassion for him
marks the best of good men.   256

59

Good people have
hard hearts, I hold,
for these cannot
be pierced at all
by the sharp arrows
of wicked words.   212

TATHĀGATENDRA SIMHA

60

The best of men alone, not others,
can bear the agitation of the mind
caused by pain and suffering:
only the diamond can withstand
friction on the mighty whetstone,
not mere lumps of clay.   291

61

Those who merit understand
find pleasure in its company,
but those who are of it devoid
can't with merit happy be.
Look, the bee comes from the forest
to the lotus in the lake,
but for the frog who lives beside it
that flower does no difference make.   253

62

The tempest uproots not the grass
softly bent to let it pass.
But mighty trees it will torment:
the great their wrath on equals vent.   261

63

Lamps illumine objects
and some people are
bright lamps of the family:
the brilliance of their merits
castes lustre on
even their forbears
who have long passed away.   258

AMRITAVARDHANA

5. Villains

64

When there are dirty things to do,
wicked minds get sharper too,
just as owls can better see
the darker it begins to be.

328

65

With a villain, influential,
mad for money, base and cruel,
holding high office, O people,
alas, where will you go?

339

KSHEMENDRA

66

As an elephant seeking shade,
tired, rests beneath a tree
and, after rest, that tree uproots:
so are the base with sanctuary.

354

67

'My luck must have been in today,
else why did he not do this earlier?
With me he has some selfish reason
or he would favour his own kin.
This lecher fears I know his secret,
if not, he would ignore me.'
Vile minds will mostly think like this
when something good is done for them.

361

KALHANA

68

The wise will with the wicked avoid
both friendliness and enmity:
in licking too, as in its biting,
the dog can cause one injury.   370

69

In the world there's nothing
more laughable than that
a wicked man describe
a good person as evil.   371

70

Having forged the villain's tongue,
so lethal for all mankind,
why did the Creator, needlessly,
make poison, fire, weaponry?   376

71

Minds poisoned by the wicked
cannot trust even the good:
the child, by hot milk scalded,
blows even on his yoghurt.   390

72

It's easy to please the ignorant,
and easier still the wise,
but even God cannot placate
one puffed up with a little knowledge.   393

BHARTRIHARI

73

Perfumed with musk and camphor,
with sandalwood and incense,
garlic still cannot give up
its inauspicious odour—
just like a base person
his inborn nature.   415

74

To fight them hurts
one's own reputation,
to seek their friendship
is a degradation;
considering both
and studying the score,
the wise must merely
the rabble ignore.   436

BHĀRAVI

75

Grind it hard, and you may get
even oil from sand;
a person mad with thirst may drink
water from a mirage; and
travellers find the rabbit's horn
if it is in their fate
but none can ever satisfy
a fool who's obdurate.   447

BHARTRIHARI

76

Seeing in himself no merit,
he wants others the same to be
and, if not, laments that in this
world no good men one can see.
He curses them and plots their ruin:
a person base, by destiny,
is filled with hankerings to score
on good people some victory.   452

VALLABHADEVA

77

A lion took the dear life
of Panini, grammar's founder;
an elephant swiftly crushed to death
Jaimini, the philosopher;
and Pingala, fount of prosody,
was killed by sharks near the seashore:
minds stricken by ignorance
have no use for merit's store.   458

6. *Niggardliness*

78

With the hoarder's money
others will toy:
it is as honey
which some amass
and others enjoy.   474

79

What you give to charity
and what you use from day to day,
that I hold your wealth to be:
the rest for someone else will stay.   475

80

Money has these courses three—
enjoyment, loss or charity;
one who will not spend or give,
with its loss is bound to live.   478

81

That villain, wealth, you guard so well,
like life itself, in secret places,
tormenting your very self,
will after death not follow you
for even the five ritual paces.   489

82

Scared it will cost money,
to friends he shows no amity.
He won't accept their favours
for fear they'll need reciprocity.
Afraid of beggars, he will lie,
he's never pleased with praise;
terrified of wealth expending,
how does a miser pass his days?   493

BHAṬṬA BĀṆA

7. Nobility

83

This is my brother, that is not—
so do the small-minded see;
for the person large of heart,
the world itself is a family.   498

BHAṬṬA UDBHAṬA

84

With constant rounds to life decreed,
both birth and death are no surprises,
but truly born is one indeed,
by whose birth the family rises.   500

85

For one blind to supplicate
is passable: he cannot see
the sneer upon the donor's face;
but can anything more painful be
than that even those who may
have their eyes for favours pray.   503

86

What is the point of wealth which is
no more than a wife in thrall,
not like the lady of the street—
enjoyable by all.   507

VIKRAMĀDITYA

87

The high-minded will let go of
their very life if needs must be
but not even the smallest favour
seek from the enemy.   513

BHAŚCHU

88

Just as a body void of life
is no more than a piece of wood,
so too, I hold, is life without
any feeling for another's good.   526

ŚANKUKA

89

One who reciprocates a favour,
no matter how much, cannot be
compared with him who rendered it
in the beginning, initially:
the first act had no ulterior cause,
the other an imitation was.   516

90

The brave and firm touch heights of glory,
of wealth though they may have no aid;
no honour in the miser's story,
even though of money made.
Behold the lion's inborn glow,
which massed merits do attain.
Can a dog that lustre show
though it wear a golden chain?   535

91

A bed of grass, a seat of stone,
shelter underneath a tree,
to drink, cool water, roots to eat,
of wild deer the company.
With all this easy, unsought wealth,
the forest has of faults but one:
supplicants are hard to find,
so scope for helping others none.
That is why we say,
there it is vain to stay.   540

ŚRI HARSHA

92

Fearing some impediment,
the base will not begin a work.
The middling start, but stop as soon
as some obstacle does them irk.
But those of highest merit,
though struck by trouble constantly,
will not abandon, even then,
the work they commenced willingly.   544

8. Allegories from Nature

93

Though borne by Shiva on his brow,
the moon looks thin and on the wane
to be dependent on another
is indeed a dreadful strain.   552

94

To another quarter it may go,
to sink in water, set in earth,
even plunge into a fire.
Yet can this lessen
the sun's great merit
in lighting up the world entire?   554

BHAṬṬA BHALLAṬA

95

The moon's splendour lasts
only till sunrise;
once that sharp-rayed
effulgence has risen,
what is the difference
between the moon and
a speck of bright cloud?   555

PRAKĀŚADATTA

96

Great lights aplenty, even the moon,
come up to ornament the sky,
but none in truth does rise or set
except the sun, whose rising is
the day and setting night.   558

97

It bestrode the highest peak
of Sumeru, lord of mountains,
dispelled darkness and pervaded
this middle world entire,
yet that moon goes down the sky
with its last few rays of light:
the rising high of even the great
is followed by decline.   561

KĀLIDĀSA

98

Without the moon,
night has no glory,
and the moon no lustre
when night is gone;
why is it then
that their full union
always happens
but once a month?   572

99

Even the radiant moon,
lord of healing herbs,
its body, nectar, its family, stars,
loses its lustre in the sun's proximity:
who is not diminished
on entering into
another's orbit?   576

100

Because it's clean and clear by nature,
its gems the ocean lets you see,
but do not therefore think the water
is no deeper than your knee.   855

101

Gems surpassing moons in glow,
the ocean casts to depths below,
and carries weeds upon its brow.
Though gems are gems, the weed a weed,
by rulers are their rules decreed.   862

PUṆYA

102

Its breakers, rising with the tide,
may smash and scatter mountain rocks;
its sound may deafen all the quarters;
it may be vast; but can the ocean
compare even with a pond
in quenching the thirst of travellers,
hot and weary with the sun?   880

103

The pure gems hidden inside are gone;
the water here is stinging brine,
unpleasing and undrinkable;
one cannot even bathe in it
for fear of sharks and serpents.
Traveller, has thirst made you mad
that, for nothing, you run towards
this wilderness called the ocean? 878

VRIDDHI

104

Look, how this lake, sole life support
for travellers, is going dry!
Fie, O cloud, you flood for nothing
the riverside market and obstruct
good people there from passing by. 834

PRAKAŚAVARSHA

105

Frogs lay in crannies, as if dead,
fish tossed and fainted in the mud,
and tortoises hid beneath the ground;
then, at that lake, a cloud unseasonal
came and such a feat performed
that, to their very necks submerged,
wild elephants now the waters drink. 843

A SOUTHERNER

106

It does not merely thunder.
It rains on time, dispels fatigue
with its showers, brings relief
to fields parched in the heat,
and gladly does all else auspicious
that the heart desires.
Its form is dense and glistening,
its advent never fails:
may this good cloud grow.   851

107

Giving shelter, yielding fruit,
of access easy, of pests free,
it exists just for the good of others,
like a noble mind, this roadside tree.   791

108

Springtime does to all the forest
foliage in abundance bring,
if the kareera tree stays leafless,
what fault is it of Spring?   794

109

The very leaves whose clusters new
provide the splendour of the tree,
it discards when they grow old—
for the base can this unusual be?   784

UPĀDHYĀYA UDAYA

110

O young champaka tree
with pleasing flowers fit to kiss
the bloom upon a young girl's cheek,
what is the use of blossoming here?
Give up the jest of florescence,
this is a desert of vulgar people.   801

NARENDRA

111

O splendid tree, with wealth of fruit!
World famous giver of relief
to the hot and hungry! From you
all I somehow got was one
small berry, half-eaten by birds,
which had fallen down.   806

112

We ate sweet fruit and slept beneath
leafy branches; drank of water
your shade had cooled; felt fresh again
and rested long with minds content.
But we are travellers, you a tree
on this road. May we meet again.   831

113

That which is the crystal's merit
itself becomes a fault:
it is so pure that it assumes
even the shade of unclean things.   894

114

The conch shell sound which echoed
that evening from a village temple
was deep, auspicious, apposite,
and pleasing to the ear.
But it was enhanced by the howls
of a fat, mad dog with neck upraised:
the imitation pleased the villagers
who drowned the sound with laughter.   915

JAYAVARDHANA

115

It has no water, trees or grass,
it wearies out the travellers;
but far from repenting
that it cannot help them,
the desert, rogue, incites them
to drink from its mirages.   943

UCHYAMĀNĀNANDA

116

Can mango trees delight one here,
with the weight of fruit bent down,
or plantain's shade to stave off heat
and champaka flowers' heady scent?
Here are just stumps of shami
on which wild camels drool,
why wander in this airless desert
and risk your life, you fool?   950

BHALLAṬA

9. *Allegories from the Animal World*

117

The lion, which always slaked its thirst
with fresh blood from the elephant's brow
ripped by the daggers of its claws,
today, alas, does beg for grass.   599

118

To Meer Shah, the baron lord,
who wished to invade Kashmir's land,
the potentate Shahabuddin
sent the following word:
'Why do you, impetuous fawn,
want to roam so carelessly?
Stop! This forest is not vacant.
In it still there is at home
the lion whose great mane, a hood
of hair, gleams with the elephant's blood.'   608-09

AMRITADATTA

119

His body, fangs and claws are small,
and, O elephant, it is true,
this is just a lion's cub,
he can't compete with you.
But such an irrepressible seed
the Creator in his heart did lay
of valour, that it must regard
even you as his rightful prey.   615

ANANDAVARDHANA

120

The lion's crowning, formally,
is never in the forest done.
Self-evident his sovereignty,
his power by his valour won.   581

121

Who is to blame, what can we do,
for this great anamoly?
The elephant's price in millions stands,
the lion's can't a penny be.   585

ŚRI MUKTĀPĪDA

122

Do not fidget, elephant-calf,
mind your manners, bow your head!
This goad, curved like the lion's claw
is too heavy to be used on you.   622

BĀNA BHAṬṬA

123

Enjoy yourself, eat lotuses,
bathe in mountain waterfalls,
your limbs carressed by loving mates;
but, elephant, give up any wish
to battle with the lord of beasts.   623

ANANDAVARDHANA

124

This elephant had gone berserk,
caused consternation all around;
how has it then been controlled
by a little mahout boy
who climbed onto his head?   624

PRAKĀŚAVARSHA

125

The dog will wag its tail, and go
grovelling down, his belly show
before his feeder; but the brave
elephant gazes long and grave
at the hand which offers bread,
and must be coaxed, before he's fed.   641

126

O proud elephant, do not keep
harking back with half-closed eyes
to those hillside forest groves;
now give up pride, accept the present,
for it is hard to control fate.   644

JALHAṆA

127

This doe lies here, unbound but still,
with an open wound, and a dart within,
not quite dead though life is ebbing:
and her stag is on the hill.   647

128

All sides roped in, the water poisoned,
nets on the ground, the forest burning,
and hunters chase it, bow in hand,
where can this king stag find refuge?   648

MUKTĀPĪḌA

129

The deer bypassed all pitfalls.
It broke the net and smashed the snare,
ran far out of the spreading flames
in the wood, with swift leaps dodging
the hunters' arrows as it fled;
but then it fell inside a well.
When fate is set against you,
what can all the effort do?   655

130

Deer, go quickly! Leave this place!
Why do you stop and turn your face,
looking back continually?
The fluttering of your eyes will not
melt even a bit these wretched hunters,
their hearts are hardened totally.   649

131

Not your dance,
a feast for the eyes,
nor your call,
elixir for the ears,
not even your tail,
a rainbow of colours—
nothing will satisfy the cat
except, O peacock, to kill you.   683

132

Brother koel, cease your song,
its music has no value now,
be quiet, sit inside some hollow
by heaps of fallen leaves concealed;
it is no more the feast of spring,
this, O friend, is winter time,
now the groves in the parks are full
of flocks of harshly cawing crows.   722

133

Here crickets chirp, there ravens crow,
here hooting cranes, there chattering apes,
yonder dreadful howls of jackals:
it's providence. How can the koel,
young and timid, raise its voice?   723

134

Standing on one stem-like leg
the aged crane retracts its neck
to give to all the little fish
the illusion of a lily bloom.   758

                              VRIDDHI

135

He can't sing sweetly like the koel,
nor has the swan's voluptuous gait
or the peacock's painted feathers:
even so the crane has weight—
and that is his hypocritical state.   761

                    ŚRI JAYAVARDHANA

136

The same in colour and in plumage,
black, in a koels' gathering
who would know it is a crow
if it did not try to sing?   764

VĀLMIKI

137

Shooing off the koel,
the crow enjoys the mango fruit;
driving out the kingly parrot,
the osprey eats the pomegranate;
the owl expels the peacock
from the treetop, and sleeps there
happily with its partner.
The eagle having gone away,
in the forest all is wrong today.   773

138

It means the sun or even the moon,
the name 'Illuminant of the Sky':
to an insect it was given
by someone pleased with the firefly.   777

139

'The moon will set
and the stars' glory fade,
the gloom-dispelling
lamps go out,
when all is dark,
I'll light it up.'
Sir firefly,
this is unlikely.   782

140

Having quaffed the lily's treasure,
there itself the youthful bee
aspires to the mimosa bud;
in this wicked honey-licker
is there any loyalty?   725

141

Amuse your fickle heart, O bee,
in other vines whose flowers can
all your rough caresses share.
Why squeeze and crush before its time
the young bud of the jasmine,
still tender and of pollen bare?   735

VIKAṬANITAMBĀ

142

He drank of nectar, as he pleased,
from the fragrant saffron bud,
spent the moonlit nights of autumn
within the lotus flower's womb,
and roamed amidst the elephants,
their temples stained with ichor flow:
how can this bee feel satisfied
on a dry kareera tree?   749

143

Kingly swan, why have you come?
Be quick, depart before it's dawn.
Here fools will take you for a crane—
they think the crane to be a swan.   704

10. Allegorical Miscellany

144

To carry loads it is not able,
nor can it serve the ploughman's need,
however the temple bull
does splendidly when at his feed.   953

145

Seated in his own abode,
the crocodile can even drown
an elephant, but on leaving it
a mere dog can bring him down.   954

146

It's better to be trampled
by the lion, on its track
with noble tail and bristling mane,
than climb upon a jackal's back.   955

147

No matter where they go, the deer
can pass their days and live
on grass of any kind;
but for lions, who eat elephants
they hunt themselves, a livelihood
is very hard to find.   957

BHAṬṬĀRKA

148

The full moon of an autumn night,
dispelling dark with myriad rays,
cannot ever match the light
of the sun, even on cloudy days.   965

149

Behold the scarecrow the farmer made
to look like him and guard the grain:
as it cannot move, the beasts are bound
to lose fear and eat the crops again.   984

150

Resting on her rounded hip,
held tight within her graceful arms,
pressed hard by the maiden's breasts,
the pitcher now enjoys the fruit
of being fired by the flames
of cow dung in the potter's kiln.   994

AMRITAVARDHANA

151

From birth insignificant, it never counted
for anything, was only trampled
underfoot into the ground each day.
Now see, friend, lifted to the skies
by a fickle wind, this very dust
sits on hillcrests and crowns of kings.   1011

152

We put up with snakes
on the sandal tree:
how can grace
unguarded be?
Tell us khadira,
is it to protect
your elegance that
these thorns you collect?   798

                                           BHALLAṬA

11. Love in Separation

153

You brush aside my hand and leave,
of strength is this a great display?
I would reckon you a man
if from my heart you got away.   1041

154

When you are not here,
I long to see you;
when you are, I fear
we will be parted.
It is no comfort—
to see you or not.   1043

155

She did not hold him by the cloak,
or bar the doorway with her arms,
fall at his feet or ask he stay:
but when on a dark and cloudy day
her husband was about to leave,
she blocked his path with streams of tears.   1057

156

If it's certain you must go,
why then the hurry, at least wait
for some more moments, while
I gaze upon your face.
Living in this world is like
water flowing down the drain,
who knows if we will meet again.   1059

157

She listened to his words, 'I'm going,'
and 'Try to manage the house,'
took note even of his return,
but hearing 'Don't be sad,' she looked
at her husband's face and sighed
and gazed at the baby at her breast.   1064

DHĪRANĀGA

158

I may have decided to go,
but how can I tell, unfeelingly,
one who is my very life?
And even telling, and then watching
her face stream with tears, and still
going: fie upon this craving for
a bit of money, such as mine.   1050

MORIKĀ

159

Stop, O friend, stop fanning me
with leaves of lotus and of palm,
the fire in my heart may just
suddenly erupt in flames.   1070

160

I do not know how to weep,
grieving too, I do not know,
these tears keep falling on their own,
I do not weep—it's truly so.   1105

161

Once again the day has passed
of your heartless father's return,
darkness now spreads on the road,
come, little son, let's go to sleep.   1106

162

O heart be still,
why suffer too,
the one you love
does not love you.   1111

163

The tie of love is gone,
the heart's assurance too,
tender feelings spent,
he's just another man.
But, thinking of the past,
dear friend, I know not why
my heart just does not shatter
into a hundred pieces.   1141

                                              VIJJĀKĀ

164

'This is black.' 'It's black, my dear.'
'Indeed it's white.' 'And why not?'
'We will go.' 'Then let us go.'
'Enough of going.' 'So be it.'
Thus he always went along
with my preference in the past,
but now he goes with someone else.
Friend, who can ever know a man?   1138

165

Somehow, in a play of pique,
I told him to get out, and he,
hard-hearted, left the bed
abruptly and just walked away.
But my shameless heart still yearns
for that callous spoiler of our love,
O good friend, what shall I do?   1143

166

'You simple girl, do you intend
to be so naive all the time?
Compose yourself and mind your honour,
don't be artless with your lover.'
Thus advised by friends, the maid
with a timorous look replies,
'Hush! Softly! My life's lord may hear you,
he is here within my heart.'   1161

AMARUKA

167

I am now by pride afflicted,
and cannot ever go to him;
nor have I clever friends who can
take me there by force or whim.
He too is proud, and will not come
on his own to look for me.
Time passes thus, and life is short,
Mother, I am sick with worry.   1160

168

One thing which he always liked
was to look at me.
He had no care for any other,
I was his life's support.
Now, look friends, I do not even
have any news of him
but live on, it is so strange
to talk about my grief.   1155

169

Go, wind, where my darling is,
touch her, come back, touch me too;
even this is a lot for lovers,
it will keep me living.   1190

VĀLMIKI MUNI

170

For a lover it's a lot to know,
and not at all of little worth,
that I and that lovely legged girl
stand upon the selfsame earth.   1191

VĀLMIKI MUNI

171

She would not e'en a garland wear
lest it should then interfere
in our lying close together:
but now between us forests lie,
rivers wide and mountains high.   1192

VĀLMIKI MUNI

172

Raising up, O just a little,
that face as lovely as a lotus—
when will I drink from it again
that incomparable elixir?   1194

VĀLMIKI MUNI

173

Her hips were round,
her movement languid,
even as she walked away,
she stepped inside my heart.   1205

ŚRI HARSHADEVA

174

The sage's word is true indeed,
that all the world is transitory:
else of parting from that doe-eyed girl
who could bear the agony?   1198

175

Even with my love-sick mind,
my sight has divine grace:
sitting here I see my love
who is in another place!   1208

DHAIRYAMITRA

176

To think of her gives fever,
to see her causes lunacy,
to touch her puts one in a swoon,
how can she my sweetheart be?   1225

177

If she, my love of graceful limbs,
lives within my heart,
how is it that it feels empty,
of fate is this a part?   1241

178

If I keep thinking of that girl,
what hope is there that I'll survive?
And if I live, forgetting her,
what is the point of staying alive?   1251

DĪPAKA

179

In the forest of her body,
in secret hills which are her breasts,
do not wander, O my mind,
there love the bandit lies in wait.   1256

180

Renunciation negates all ills—
this seems to be a pack of lies,
all my ills began when I
renounced that girl with innocent eyes.   1271

ŚŪDRAKA

181

She covered her lips
with her fingers again
as she timidly warned me
that I should refrain.
I lifted her face,
she turned to my shoulder,
I do not know why
I did not then kiss her.   1273

KĀLIDĀSA

182

Even today,
I remember her face,
pale, and brushed
by swinging earrings,
with beads of sweat
appearing like pearls
in love's exertion,
as my darling strove
to act the man.   1291

BILHAṆA

183

I do not know who will be fated
to enjoy this faultless beauty,
an unsmelt flower, a bud unpicked,
an unpierced pearl, fresh honey whose
flavour none has tasted.   1332

KĀLIDĀSA

184

She grieves in my sorrow,
thrills in my joy,
suffers my anguish,
and speaks sane words
when mine are incensed.
She knows the times,
is clever in speech,
delights in my praise.
Noble adviser,
comrade and helper,
my wife is many
things rolled in one.   1353

BHĀSA

185

She is in the bloom of youth,
my mind has gone haywire:
her limbs are full of loveliness,
in mine there spreads a fire.   1212

AMARUKA

186

I saw my angry sweetheart
in a dream today.
'Do not touch me!' she exclaimed
in tears, about to go away.
As I began assuring her
with sweet words and an embrace deep,
just then, O friend, a wicked fate
robbed me of my sleep.   1362

NIDRĀDARIDRA

12. *Friends and Go-betweens*

187

You simple girl, why try to hide
the pain of parting from your lover
by holding back your tears?
Your pillow, drenched night after night,
now put out to dry, tells all.   1095

188

Your face is pale, eyes bright with tears,
limbs gaunt, gait dull, composure gone.
Don't be coy, you foolish girl,
why not tell me, your best friend,
the truth of what, within the hour,
has brought you to this pass?   1096

189

Your gaze is languid, soft with love,
you shut your eyes repeatedly
and open them for just a moment
to stare, or shyly dart a glance
full of some inner feeling.
Tell me, young miss, who is he,
that lucky man you are looking at?   1098

190

If that heartless man has gone,
ignoring these flashing eyes
and the girdle clinging to your hips,
it's he who is the loser.   1168

191

When your sweetheart came, you did not
greet him straightaway and long,
nor put your arms around him and
speak sweetly words dripping with love
or, gathered to your upthrust bosom,
hold him in a deep embrace:
you simpleton, you have been let down
by your own ineptness.   1173

RATNAMITRA

192

What did you get by being
so fickle and self-willed?
He came to your house,
fell at your feet so lovingly,
and you ignored him!
Now you'll never be happy
and weep lifelong
reaping the fruit of anger.   1176

AMARUKA

193

True, today is Tuesday,
not suitable for you;
even so, messenger, go,
a sufferer cannot wait.   1179

194

Good times are as waves on water,
youth is but a moment's span,
life is frail—an autumn cloud,
go quick, messenger, tell him this.   1180

195

Messenger, it's getting dark,
that rake is young, you just a girl,
the message secret, the place a wood,
the spring breeze sets all minds awhirl.
Still, go, and may the meeting spell
good news for me. God guard you well.   1188

                                   ŚĪLĀ BHAṬṬĀRIKĀ

196

'Where is the question
of any quarrel?
She lives for you,
her eyes on the door,
head bowed on hand.'
Such words, repeated
to the lover,
give him new pleasure
every time.   1182

                                          BHĀRAVI

197

Do not get concerned, or worry
that she is so young, thin and delicate.
Have you ever seen a vine
shed flowers when a bee alights?
So, sir, in some lonely spot,
show no mercy, kiss her hard:
the sugar-cane stem will never yield
its juice if handled softly.   1401

                                     VIKAṬANITAMBĀ

198

O hard of heart, she could not bear
the pangs of separation, and
as she gave up life, has sent
this final message meant for you:
'A child to give me funeral water,
luckless I leave just one daughter.
Do not give her off in marriage
to one engrossed in work abroad.'   1403

BRAHMAYAŚASVĀMIN

199

Wayfarer, brother, go home quickly,
I have seen your darling there:
eager for some word of you
she meets each traveller on the road,
but, choked with tears, she cannot speak
and only sighs escape her lips
as, head bent low, she weeps and weeps.   1409

200

Pure cheek on palm,
eyes on the road,
her heart with you:
since long it has been thus,
how could she
have time to stand
on dignity?   1381

VARARUCHI

201

Her hot sighs evoke the summer;
a flow of tears, the monsoon time;
pale and sunken breasts, the autumn;
the two winters, her face sublime,
now trembling, now a fading lotus;
then beads of sweat come like spring days.
In missing you, it is a marvel,
all the seasons she displays.   1406

                                        HARIGAṆA

202

'Messenger, did you go?' 'I did,
my lady, to that libertine.'
'Did you see him long? What was
he doing?' 'He was just amusing
himself, playing on the vina.'
'Fortune's made him proud. What did
he say?' 'He did not speak at all.'
'Because of pride?' 'No, choked by tears.'
'The rogue! Those are his tricky ways.'   1424

203

Messenger, your face and bosom,
with your hand why cover more?
Lips and breasts, like soldiers brave,
look best while bearing marks of war.   1428

204

Why talk about it more, messenger?
For my work's accomplishment
you gave of even your own flesh,
what to say of other things?   1434

                                        VARARUCHI

205

The other night, in course of love,
somehow he stole a cloak of mine.
You have now retrieved it by
giving away your own!
Can any messenger be as clever
as you in covering up a slip?   1437

BĪJAKA

206

'Why do you pant?' 'I came back fast.'
'What makes you thrill?' 'He has agreed.'
'Your hair's undone.' 'I fell at his feet.'
'Your skirt knot too!' 'From going and
coming.'
'There's sweat on your face.' 'I went in the
heat.'
'You seem worn out.' 'I talked a lot.'
'But, what do you have to say, messenger,
of your lips, which seem to look
like faded lotus buds?'   1440

ŚILĀ BHAṬṬĀRIKĀ

207

Your hair is mussed, your cheeks are pink,
all your frame is trembling too.
It does seem to me, my lady,
that my lover has beaten you!   1435

JAYAMĀDHAVA

208

Lover, you deserve this paragon,
and she deserves you equally—
the moon shines not without the night,
and a moonless night must dismal be.   1396

                                 MORIKĀ

13. Beautiful Women

209

In this worthless scheme of things
the treasure she will always be—
a fawn-eyed girl of languid grace
to whom love comes spontaneously.   1453

210

The dark-eyed maiden's wavy tresses
stream between her rounded breasts
like a line of bees on their way
to the heart, suffused with the nectar
of a freshly blooming lotus.   1484

                              PUṆYA

211

That beauty spot upon your forehead
glitters like an arrow's blade;
fixing it on those archéd eyebrows,
miss, who are you about to slay?   1488

212

How has that pair of dark-blue lilies
blossomed on your lotus face?
Is this a portent of some trouble
which will of good men leave no trace?   1492

213

Though flowers growing in a flower
is neither seen nor heard of ever,
miss, on the lotus of your face
of lilies blue I see a brace.   1495

214

Your lower lip, with coral glow,
is a desert trail, fair maid,
whose heart will it not overcome
with thirst and longing for a drink?   1507

215

Nectar, no doubt, has its flavour;
honey too; what can one say,
fresh mango juice is also sweet;
but a discriminating person may
sit in judgement and pronounce,
even once, if indeed there
is any taste more luscious than
of the lips of one's beloved here.   1511

216

It cannot make itself resemble
my love's sweet face in any way:
the moon expands and then reduces
its orb repeatedly, to this day.   1517

ŚRI HARSHA

217

Her full breasts are lotus blooms,
dark nipples like two bees upon them,
the stem, a hair line to the navel,
points to the treasure trove below.   1545

218

O you rash daredevil girl!
Why go whirling round and round?
Sit down! Or else your waist will snap
with the swirling of your breasts.   1547

VIKAṬANITAMBĀ

14. Pride and Placation

219

I frown, I no more look for him,
speak little, and shroud myself
with a cloak. The mind alone
wanders, anguished. But who
can divine that? So, hurry,
fetch the man I love, to see
how I have been wounded.   1579

220

Even as I frown, the eyes
search for him more eagerly.
I keep silent, still a smile
flits across this wretched face.
The mind I've steeled, but even so
my body bristles by itself.
When I see him, how indeed,
will I stand upon this pride?   1580

BHADANTA ĀROGYA

221

My wayward eyes may flit and roam,
this wretched girdle slip, this bodice
rip with the heaving of my breasts,
but, friend, I'll never speak again
to that rogue of a lover, that is
if with wounded pride my heart
does not just then burst apart.   1575

AMARUKA

222

When my lover at last appeared,
after long, and suddenly,
deliberately I shut my eyes
and did not speak as he would like.
But my arms did not obey me.
They bristled and embraced him hard
as, by practice, they were wont.
Mother, what then could I do?   1582

223

As he approached her
she got up in welcome,
leaving no chance for
their sitting together;
avoided his embrace
on the pretext of going
to fetch him a betel leaf;
and did not converse,
keeping busy with servants
in the vicinity.
She was thus courteous
to her lover, but clever
enough, nevertheless,
to show her displeasure.   1583

PULINA

224

She did not ignore courtesy,
frown, be terse or contrary,
nor say anything impolite,
but when her lover clasped her in
a close embrace, her eyes welled up
with tears and made her anger known.   1587

DHARMAKĪRTI

225

You hold my life
like a ball in your hand;
how long, fair maid,
do you want this game
of changing moods
to continue?   1593

ŚAŚIVARDHANA

226

'Beautiful, give up this pride.
Look at me, I'm at your feet.
You've never been so cross before.'
By her husband thus addressed,
she cast a glance from half-closed eyes,
shed many tears, said not a word.   1600

227

Your eyes he made of lilies blue,
your face of lotus flowers,
your teeth of jasmine buds, your lips
of young and fresh red shoots,
and your limbs of champaka blooms.
With all this, darling, how could God
possibly make your heart of stone?   1610

228

The night is almost past,
the crescent moon is turning pale,
the lamp is flickering, as if it
also wants to fall asleep.
Though I have begged forgiveness
you are still enraged.
By nearness to your breasts, you minx,
has your heart also turned hard?   1612

BĀNA BHATTA

229

O you lovely legged girl,
why do you hide and peep?
Look at your sweetheart openly:
water drunk in droplets
dripping from a blade of grass
will never quench your thirst.   1596

VRISHNIGUPTA

230

'Girl!' 'My lord,' 'Stop being angry.'
'What have I done in anger?'
'You're cross with me.' 'It's not your fault,
all the faults are only mine.'
'Then why weep and choke with sobs?'
'In front of whom do I do so?'
'Why, me.' 'And who am I to you?'
'My love.' 'I'm not, and so I weep.'   1614

BHATTA KUMĀRA

231

O proud beauty, hard of heart,
stop being angry! It ruins pleasure,
is wrong, when youth and being together
are so fleeting. Death counts each
passing day, and love is not
complete without a quarrel!   1619

BHĀSA

232

In the beginning were those days
when you and I were one.
Then you, the lover, I became
simply a mistress losing hope.
Now you are husband, I the spouse,
what more is there to say?
My spirits turned as hard as rock,
and this the fruit I reap today.   1622

233

'It is as you say, my lady,
all the faults are always mine,
though what offence, O lotus-eyes,
can there ever be from husbands?
Yet here I am, with folded hands,
punish your slave at will.'
'When a slave has crimes committed
can there be scope for pardon still?'   1631

234

Take a field of powdered sugar,
on which clouds have honey rained,
the seedlings then manure with candy
and irrigate with juice of grapes:
if that bore fruit, its superlative
sweetness would then match your voice.   1639

235

Kama struck me with his arrows,
I did not care as I recalled
you to be my healing balm;
nor did separation's fire
burn me, as the hope of meeting
you was with me as a charm;
I passed those days in making
wonderful resolves withal—
you know them as you're in my heart,
a witness to them all.   1634

SŪRAVARMAN

15. The Seasons

Spring

236

This hum is not a swarm of bees,
from inebriety its sweet note born:
it is the sound of Kama's bow,
in this season being drawn.   1644

BHĀMAHA

237

Embracing the mango blossom
the bee kisses it with much ado
as a lover would his sweetheart,
thrilled at meeting her anew.   1647

238

In the woodland, everywhere,
the flame of the forest trees have shed
all their leaves, their branches bent
with flowers bright as blazing fires,
and the earth gleams in the spring
like a new bride in red attire.   1678

KĀLIDĀSA

239

The koel's call does now proclaim
at the love god's own command:
'Travellers, do not leave your homes,
give up thoughts of going away;
proud ladies, do not be so difficult,
why get angry with your lovers?
For spring, which can consume the lives
of parted couples, has arrived.'   1689

Summer

240

The lane is empty and deserted
in the searing heat of summer,
but for the couple there, absorbed
in talking only with each other,
the sun shines like the moon.   1693

241

Fearing the unbearable heat
of the sun, now at its zenith,
shadows too, in search of shade,
have withdrawn beneath the tree.   1699

ŚRIMAD AVANTIVARMAN

242

Troubled by the sun's hot rays,
scorched by the pathway's burning sand,
panting, uncoiled, hood contracted,
the snake now rests beneath the peacock.   1703

243

To feel the cool breeze on a body
covered with drops of perspiration;
to taste the water, cold and clear,
in a mouth all parched with thirst;
'after travelling far, to rest
the tired limbs beneath the shade:
blessed indeed is one who spends
the summer wandering in Kashmir.   1710

BHAṬṬA BĀṆA

244

If you wish to get home quickly,
having pined each day to see
your dear wife with her swinging hairbraid,
then, friend, though you may thirsty be,
from that well for drinking water
it's better you keep far away,
for the artless, languid glances
of the girl who tends it
get travellers there to stay.   1712

245

Seeing the forest all around
inhospitable, as if on fire,
and fearful of the heat, the buffalo
drinks acrid water from the pond
boiling in the midday sun,
and tries to curl its body so
as to shelter in its own shadow.   1706

MĀTRISHEṆA

The Rains

246

O cloud! Thunder, rain, or throw
bolts of lightning down below!
Men on their way their girls to meet
do not think of cold or heat.   1724

247

The sky is like a madman,
it dances with arms of lightning,
laughs with a flight of cranes
and weeps with streams of rain.   1725

248

Mountain peaks, with water streaming
from rainbow clouds which rest on them,
seem like rutting elephants draped
in cloaks of many colours.   1728

VIŚĀKHADEVA

249

Dark clouds above
and sloping hills
where peacocks dance,
the ground below
all white with new blooms,
where can the traveller
rest his gaze?   1744

BHARTRIHARI

250

The air I breathe is bitter
with the scent of mountain jasmine,
I hear the clouds thundering,
have spent night after night
on a lonely bed
trying in vain to sleep,
covered the walls with signs
to mark the passage of time,
but you never come
and this life is hard to end.   1764

251

With sky as pit, and lightning's fire,
Kama performs the ceremony
for causing turmoil in the hearts
of women parted from their lovers:
the thunder is his litany.   1780

ŚRI RĀJĀNAKA ŚUGA

252

The sky is dark with clouds,
dark as the smoke from fires,
the ground is spread with grass
sprouting fresh, dark green;
the time is indeed suited
for making love, it comes
when for separated couples
the one refuge is death.   1760

CHIĀKA

253

Let clouds thunder
and stream rain,
lightning flash,
winds blow their coldest;
I have an antedote
to stave off fear,
it is my sweetheart
reclining on my chest.   1790

Autumn

254

In autumn, as their flow recedes,
rivers gradually reveal
their sandy banks, like girls still shy
of making love, the inner thigh.   1792

VĀLMIKI

255

Autumn comes, a bride in white,
her visage radiant as the moon,
with eyes like petals of blue lilies,
and a wealth of lotus flowers,
a wild goose by her side—
good fortune's goddess, praised in song.   1818

MAHĀMANUSHYA

256

With rich grain and blooming lotus,
lucid waters, song of cranes,
the moon's bright disc, the sky's expanse,
autumn, and its many faces,
win the hearts of all mankind.   1823

257

The sun is sharp and hot,
like the base with new wealth.
The deer shed horns
like an ingrate his friends.
The waters grow limpid
like the mind of a sage,
and mud starts drying up
like a poor man who's lustful.   1821

BHĀSA

258

Rice stalks, heavy now with grain,
are slowly bending down their heads
as if to smell the lotus flowers
growing beside them in the field.   1805

VARARUCHI

Early Winter

259

'She is the sweetheart
of the sun, my enemy':
and the frost, in anger,
has blighted the lily.   1830

BILHANA

260

O winter, as you pass, for me
two things will memorable prove:
the water freezing on its own,
and nights ideal for making love.   1836

261

In a little grass cottage,
beside the barley field,
on a bed of fresh-cut straw,
sleep the farmer couple;
so well protected are they
by the warmth of her breasts
that the cold keeps far away.   1840

KAMALĀYUDHA

Late Winter

262

The door of the room shut tight,
a fire burning by the bed,
an ample quilt to cover you,
in your arms a loving spouse:
to a person who sleeps thus,
what can the snowfall do?   1853

BĀṆA

263

It was dusk. At first the traveller
sat by a public bonfire and,
not caring if he got scorched,
warmed himself to heart's content.
Then, partly covered with a rag,
he slept beneath the thatched roof
in a corner of the shrine
of the village goddess, till
a wind, laden with snowflakes,
drove him to another corner.   1857

16. Nightfall

264

The sun sinks fast, as if afraid
of angry glares by lovelorn women
who await with trembling lips
this signal for nocturnal trysts.   1897

NARENDRA

265

Pure or sullied, firm or fickle,
straight or curved—each quality
is by darkness made the same;
evil's force, it is a shame,
overwhelms variety.   1901

KĀLIDĀSA

266

The sun, in setting, seems to say,
its last ray on the lily's head:
'I go, fair one, my time is up.
Sleep, tomorrow I will come
to awaken you myself.'   1908

ŚRI HARSHADEVA

267

The sharp-rayed sun, some people say,
sinks in the sea at the end of day;
it goes to light another world—
this is what some others hold;
and yet others do proclaim,
it merges with some cosmic flame.
But all of this seems just a lie—
it has no witness standing by.
As for me, I'm sure, dear friend,
that the sun, when day does end,
within some maiden's heart must stay
to burn it while her lover's away.   1902

INDULEKHĀ

268

As the sun sets in the western hills,
a full moon rises on the crest
of the mountain in the east:
the glory of the evening sky
resembles Hara dancing, with
two copper cymbals in his hands.   1909

269

Moonlight is maddening,
it turns the world upon its head:
the cat licks it in the cup like milk;
the elephant reaches for the beams
filtering through leaf-laden trees,
mistaking them for tender shoots;
and the girl thinks it's her garment
on the bed, at love's end.   1994

BHĀSA

270

Parting the dark mass of her hair
with the fingers of his rays,
closing the lotus blooms, her eyes,
the moon kisses the face of Night.   1963

KĀLIDĀSA

271

That lily's life were passed in vain,
which did not the moon behold;
the moon's existence fruitless too,
if it did not ever see
the lily waken and unfold.   1964

BILHAṆA AND THE PRINCESS

272

That ancient poet is a fool.
A curse upon his poetry
which compares a woman's face
with the moon. How can that be?
The eyebrows arched, the sidelong glance,
the rage, the laughter full of glee—
in the moon with just its rabbit,
where can anyone ever see?   1977

273

Moon-faced girl, look at the moon,
an earring for the maiden, night,
a lotus petal in sky's lake,
a flint for honing Kama's arrow.   1984

274

Trees look like royal parasols,
hills like the snowy Mount Kailasa,
mud as curds, as milk the sea,
vines like pearl strings, fruit like shells:
all the land's expanse is turned
white with the rising of the moon.   2002

BHAṬṬA TRIVIKRAMA

275

The road is dark, she trembles so,
her lover stole her heart away,
how will you lead her to his house,
Kama, can you ever say?   1936

276

Midnight, dark and cloudy skies,
the city lanes deserted,
the husband gone to foreign lands,
give joy supreme to a wanton.   1937

277

'Where are you going, pretty maid,
in this dark of midnight?'
'Where lives my lover, dear to me
even more than my life.'
'Are you not afraid, my girl,
of setting forth alone?'
'A warrior with his feathered arrows,
Madana goes with me.'   1946

AMARUKA

278

The necklace glitters on your breast,
the girdle chimes around your hips,
and anklets tinkle on your feet;
when you are going out to meet
your lover with so much fanfare,
why do you, O innocent maid
cast furtive glances everywhere? 1947

ARGAṬA

17. Carousals

279

She, who was cross
with her faithless lover
and would not relent
when he fell at her feet,
is now, with wine,
no more fastidious,
and satisfies him
as she did before.   2014

NAGNAJITA

280

The moon could not compete
with the glow on this beauty's face
and, ashamed, it's gone
to swim within her wine-filled glass
and gain a purer form.   2015

BHĀRAVI

281

Though she drank much wine,
she did not get drunk
out of concern her lover
may turn to another woman.
Inebriation requires
the mind to be relaxed.   2010

282

On the pretext of drinking wine,
the young couple, their mouths together,
are pouring out, in fact, the juice
of love into one another's heart.   2016

JAYAMĀDHAVA

283

How can a half-drunk glass of wine
glitter so? Well, that young woman
kissed it with her pretty red
lips and filled it with their glow.   2017

JAYAMĀDHAVA

284

'In this pleasure bower there
is a jasmine vine whose lovely
flowers none have plucked so far':
saying this, and softly taking
the innocent maid by hand, a rogue
led her to that lonely spot.   1866

JAYAMĀDHAVA

285

The bees forsake the vine whose blooms
have already been gathered, and
go to girls who wear them in garlands:
the wicked think only of themselves.   1863

286

The girl beheld a drop of water
roll upon a lotus leaf
and, as if it were a pearl,
stretched out her hand to get it.   1875

VALLABHADEVA

287

Wet skirts now cling to women's hips,
the girdle strings so soaked in water
that their bells have fallen silent,
like stars turned pale in the moonlight.   1873

18. Love in Union

288

Should I merge within your limbs,
or in myself absorb you?
After long I have you back
and don't know what to do.   2027

289

Tell me truly, O my love,
what is it you do to me:
to hear you is a real pleasure,
to see you is pure ecstacy.   2038

290

The bees are after you, my lady,
they think your eyes are lilies blue,
your lips the crimson phoenix flower,
hands lotuses, cheeks blossoms true,
your dark tresses they think to be
their own kin and very dear:
it's hard to fend off their embraces,
what all will you guard out here?   2037

291

In two lovers' game of dice
the wager was a kiss,
who the stake has won or lost—
only Manmatha knows this.   2048

JAYAVARDHANA

292

'Wait a bit! Let go my skirt!
Others will wake! O you are shameless!
At least put out the light, I beg you!'
These words of my beloved
enthral me more
than even the act of love.   2053

RĀJAPUTRA PARPAṬI

293

She hurries to leave our room with friends,
lowers her eyes when I look at her,
will not reply when spoken to,
turns her back to me in bed,
and trembles when embraced:
the newly wed bride is dear to me
by this very contrariety.   2072

ŚRI HARSHADEVA

294

Though they hide the heart's desire
to begin making love,
the couple understand each other
just by fleeting glances.   2044

KAYYAṬA

295

Newly married brides are full of longing
when they are far, but then feel shy
near their husbands, and afraid
when trembling on the bed they lie.   2047

RUDRAṬA

296

It stole the joy from conversation,
and pre-empted intercourse—
when the lover's eyes were overcome
by sleep, suddenly and perforce.   2050

297

When neglect is itself devotion,
and not looking an ardent gaze,
silence, too, a glad communion,
then love, deep hidden, shows its face.   2051

298

Her husband has just returned
from a difficult crossing of the desert.
The woman gazes at his face,
her eyes moist with relief,
and softly brushes, with her own sash,
his camel, as she gives it fodder.   2075

299

She was offended, lay in bed
with limbs inert, her back to him;
he, from behind, with gentle hand,
caressed her softly round the navel;
she broke into a sweat of passion,
her girdle slipped, but angry still,
she heaved a cunning put-on sigh
and loosened the knot of her skirt.   2085

300

'Do you think she does not know
who has come and closed her eyes?
Why stand behind her? It is pointless,
your limbs are bristling, and she knows.
Leave her, you fool, don't you see
the teardrops trickling down her face?'
Her friend spoke thus, and hastily
the youth embraced the girl.   2068

301

Parted for ages, weak with longing,
to meet again was so delightful
that all the world seemed born anew.
The day was long, somehow it passed,
and when night came, the couple spent
more time in talking, than in making love.   2063

302

She clings? She melts?
She sleeps? She's dead?
A hundred doubts assail me
with my darling in my arms.   2088

303

Blessed be the mumblings
of 'yes' and 'no' within her mouth
as the lover grasps her hair,
lifts up the face and forcibly
kisses the haughty girl.   2090

VIJJĀKĀ

304

The faltering voice, the sibilant sound,
the trembling hands, the half-closed eyes,
of women, in love-making's course,
turn into Madana's weaponry.   2092

BHĀRAVI

305

Capriciousness and lack of shame,
obstinacy and impudence,
the unpitying and passionate heart,
of calm and steadfastness no sense:
all these, not faults, but virtues prove
in the act of making love.   2095

BHAṬṬA PARIBHŪTA

306

'Master! Lord! My darling! Hold me!
Hold me close! O you are wicked!
Cruel! Thinking of your own pleasure!
You hurt me! Stop! Enough! Enough!'
Such words of women in making love
are signs of their affection.   2096

BHAṬṬA KUMĀRA

307

After love, he made pretence
of sleeping, when she kissed him
but realized he was awake
as all his body bristled.
'You must be punished for this deceit!'
Saying this, she bit his lip
and got what she was after.   2102

308

At love's end, that charming girl
gropes for her garment everywhere,
at the flaming lamp a flower flings,
and confused, with a little laugh,
tries to close her husband's eyes,
then at last, to his arms returns.   2105

309

Lying in the same bed,
their faces turned away;
not replying, ill at ease,
wishing at heart to make up,
but conscious of their dignity.
At long last a sidelong glance,
a meeting of the eyes,
and the ice is broken:
the couple laugh, and swiftly
passion reignites.   2112

310

Now the girdle tinkles,
the anklet bells are stilled;
this must be a lucky lover
whose darling acts the man.   2122

311

May they fall upon your breast,
the beads of perspiration, trickling
from that lusty lass's face
in heat of love, with roles reversed.   2119

312

He grasps her hair, his eyes riveted
on the spot between her thighs,
and she, the minx, well skilled in love,
kisses her lover on the mouth.   2125

JAYAMĀDHAVA

313

I said, 'My dear, I'll be your girl,
you be the man.' The doe-eyed maid
shook her head, 'No! Never! No!'
Then took a bracelet off her wrist,
and fastening it on mine, she gave
assent without a word.   2127

314

Here sprinkled with betel juice,
there besmeared with aloe paste,
here a spread of scented powder,
there red lacquer from the feet,
strewn with flowers spilt and scattered
by the dishevelment of hair,
the bedspread all the scenes recounts
of a woman making love.   2123

315

Sugar candy, betel leaf,
milk and butter, children's sound,
a maiden's glance, a poet's fancy:
these O Shakra, king of heaven,
in your domain will not be found.   2138

316

Friend, you're very fortunate
to be able to narrate
the sweet exchanges full of joy
in meetings with your lover boy.
For, when his hand my darling placed
on the skirt knot at my waist,
I swear I cannot then recall
any, anything at all.   2142

317

Lips with colour kissed away,
eyes bereft of kohl,
tresses straggling on the face:
but at dawn, contented,
their glory is more
than of the night before,
when merely ornamented.   2139

BHARTRISVĀMIN

318

When to the bed my lover came
my skirt knot opened by itself—
I held the cord, but the dress slipped off
with just a bit left on my hips.
That is all I know, dear friend,
for when he took me in his arms,
who was he and I myself,
or how we two made love together,
I don't at all remember.   2147

AMARUKA

319

As the moon was kissing dawn
he saw her lord, the sun, appear,
quickly then he hid himself,
turning pale with fear.   2155

MUKTIKOSHTHAKA

320

At day-breaking, as I watched,
the dark veil of the lady, night,
was by the sun's ray-hands removed,
and the moon despoiled of light.   2154

PUNYA

321

Ignoring his entreaty,
she turned her back,
pretended to sleep.
In time, she hears
the cock's loud crowing
and turning over,
her eyes full of slumber
and still half-closed,
the woman embraces
the lord of her life.   2175

MĀGHA

322

The horses wake and, softly neighing,
search for grass on every side,
the cock too waves its copper plume
and sounds a note, both high and sweet,
which lovers hear most angrily.   2168

323

Set to leave the trysting chamber
now that night was almost over,
she kissed and embraced him
but was not contented;
with one foot on the floor, the other
still in bed, that slender maid
put her arms around her lover
and gave him a long, long kiss.   2191

324

It inspires the poet's muse,
makes palace pigeons chirp,
and enrages husbands
of all beautiful women:
it is the trumpet's call at daybreak,
and the clanging chains of elephants
as they arise from dusty beds,
the noise filling the sky.   2223

RĀJAŚEKHARA

325

When the pet parrot of the house,
which heard at night the couple's love-talk,
began repeating it in front
of the elders in the morning,
the bride, embarrassed and aghast,
took a ruby from her eardrop
and, pretending to the bird,
that it was a pomegranate seed,
stuffed the gem inside its beak
to stop it prattling any more.   2214

19. Miscellaneous Verses: 1

326

'Doctor, what would you advise
as medicine for one stricken by
that slender maiden's flashing eyes?'
'The best, an embrace I regard:
grab her hair and kiss her hard.'   2225

327

The arched eyebrow, the flitting glance,
cunning, sidelong and delightful,
the tender mien, the bashful laugh,
the languid grace of pause and motion:
these are the ornaments of women,
and their weapons too.   2227

TWO KAVIPUTRAS

328

I am alone, a weak young girl,
in this house. The master has
gone away to foreign lands.
Foolish traveller, whom will you ask
if you can stay here? My infirm
old mother-in-law is deaf and blind.   2234

RUDRAṬA

329

The virgin is merely curious,
the widow just seeks friction,
the harlot wants a bit of money,
one's spouse has no other option.
The reasons, for which women want
men, are a vast variety;
it needs good karma to get another's
bride, purely out of amity.   2238

330

I speak the truth, there is no bias.
This is a fact. In all the world,
than girls there is naught more enchanting,
nor more unique a source of pain.   2231

331

The bashful glances at each other,
the words sent through a message bearer
to meet tomorrow or today,
loving, joyous, all the way,
and when the meeting does take place,
the ardent kisses and embrace:
this is Kama's harvest true—
the rest even the animals do.   2237

332

Fresh made ghee, and milk with ice,
turmeric, a new shawl's drape,
red saffron, aruka fruit and turasi,
wood apples, honey and the grape,
a Kira lass with limbs as tender
as lotus buds: I have to say
a Kashmiri who knows not these,
I think had better silent stay.   2243

333

A mango grove, a fragrant breeze,
the ground a dark-green lawn of grass,
a lute's soft sound, a cup of wine
stirred with jasmine buds, a tranquil
moonlit night, and sidelong glances
from a girl with lovely lotus eyes—
what else is worthwhile in a world
as fleeting as the lightning's flash?   2251

MANGALAVATSA

334

Till then only does man stay
on the course of virtue's way,
keep his urges in control,
of shame and decorum know the role:
till, from brows drawn to the ear,
the arrow of some wanton glance
released, dark-winged, his heart will tear,
and rob him of his resistance.   2246

DHARMAKĪRTI

335

Where is the cloud, and where the peacock
with its fan of brilliant feathers?
Where the pure-rayed moon, and where
the waves upon the ocean's waters?
Behold the rising sun, and see
the lotus ringed with bees so gay:
one who loves another, pleases
the heart from even far away.   2240

20. The Heroic Mode

336

Into battle as I go,
this I swear and firmly vow:
the enemy force will never see
the hind side of my cavalry.
I cannot promise any more:
fate is fickle, and in war
both defeat and victory
must depend on destiny.   2275

CHANDAKA

337

Many study law books,
even the one-legged can;
but one who will bear
the sharp-edged stroke
of the enemy's sword—
such a man is rare.   2255

RĀJAPUTRA ARGAṬA

338

Earth, be still!
O serpent, hold her!
Tortoise king, support them both!
And to steady all the three,
you cosmic elephants, be prepared:
the prince now draws great Shiva's bow.   2282

FROM BĀLARĀMĀYAṆA

339

When trampled on, it rises up
and engulfs the trampler's head—
even that dust is better than
the much humiliated man
who just will not react.   2264

MĀGHA

340

So long his honour is intact,
till then truly he's a man,
good fortune will wait upon him
and glory with him stay.   2266

BHĀRAVI

341

Mount Meru's peak is not too high,
nor the nether world too low,
or even the sea uncrossable—
but only for determined men.   2260

21. *Humour and Satire*

342

To raise the fallen,
and make the risen fall:
your powers strange, vagina,
seem supernatural.   2293

VYĀGHRAGAṆA

343

Proudly struts the yokel,
sash around the waist,
flashing his underskirt,
jabbering for a penny's sake.   2295

344

Widows are caught up with gigolos,
and housewives with their husbands,
whores want only wealthy men,
students make do with the hand.   2296

345

It's women's eyes
which do the flirting;
but it all ends up
at an innocent spot
between the legs.   2297

346

Pliant to start with,
then turning stiff,
ruthless in business,
and when it is done
all soft again:
merchants, in life,
are just like the penis.   2298

347

Many thorns the rose surround,
lilies bloom in muddy ground,
each charmer has a go-between:
fault-free gems are seldom seen.   2299

348

There is no fear
your palate will split
or your tongue be pulled out;
so, freely speak:
a man loquacious
is deemed perspicacious.   2300

349

Faulty words are deer, afraid
of the lion which is grammar;
where could they hide, if not within
the depths of all those mouths cavernous
of gurus, clowns, astrologers,
physicians and vedic priests?   2301

350

The astrologer may calculate
the moon's union with a star
but, alas, is unaware
who his good wife's lovers are.

2302

351

It's sinful to go for another's wife,
one's own does not exist;
so, much praised by men well raised
is the beauty held in one's fist.

2303

352

The fair and fetching plump expanse
of that whore's depilated pubes
is like the golden slope of Meru
grazed clean by stallions of the sun.

2304

353

'This is my rice,
and this my wheat,
these my lovely beans.'
While man thus bleats,
'mine, mine, mine, mine,'
in voice caprine,
he's taken away by death.

2306

354

Who indeed can call him clever?
The Creator was a fool—
he made no oil in pumpkins
nor on elephants wool.

2307

355

Of planets he's the tenth, located
in the daughter's sign for good,
always difficult and demanding,
a drain upon your livelihood:
in the horoscopes they draw
he is the proverbial son-in-law.   2308

356

Death laughs at him
who guards his health,
the world at him
who hoards his wealth,
and she laughs too—
the adultrous wife,
at her husband, guarding
the son like his life.   2309

357

This serpent's mouth
is down below,
with a single tooth
and a lethal flow
which has no cure.
It's called vagina
and it has bitten
all men for sure.   2310

358

Fool, when getting food for free,
for life do not so cautious be:
free food is difficult to obtain,
life, with rebirth, will come again.   2311

359

For comfort in their afterlife
parents pray for children, who
will send them clotted cream in heaven,
with poached and roasted pheasant too.   2313

360

A mouth which is not occupied
with helpful words for some poor soul,
with savouring betel or kissing lips,
is no better than the nether hole.   2316

361

Drink from wayside water tanks,
eat at the public table,
sleep inside a place of worship,
fuck wherever you are able.   2317

362

It was summer,
the priest was asleep
beneath a tree,
a dog appeared
and pissed on his hand,
he muttered the words
for taking a fee.   2318

363

Salutations, my lord doctor,
you dispatch men without exception;
giving you this onerous duty,
Death enjoys a fine vacation.   2319

MAYA

364

The physician has no mastery
over how long life will be.
All his physic
just therein lies:
he robs the sick,
from the dead he flies. 2320

MAYA

365

'Doctor, I am weak with fever,
say what is the remedy.'
'Drink a cup of some strong liquor
and bring another one for me.' 2321

MAYA

366

Sages, themselves prone to anger,
teach others not to angry be,
like paupers who, to make a living,
preach the merits of alchemy. 2323

HARSHA

367

If the clerk could never eat
his mother's flesh while in her womb,
the only reason for this feat
was: at the time he had no teeth. 2326

368

With quill tucked behind his ear,
the clerk you must not trust;
better do so with black serpents
or wild tigers, if you must. 2327

369

The deer of bad language,
killed by lions of grammar,
were eaten by actors and doctors,
and pale men from another land.   2333

370

With some skill at this or that,
man attains the princely caste
where in cursing lies his merit,
his manliness in fashions fast.   2335

PRAKĀŚAVARSHA

371

Friend, listen to this wondrous deed
a rustic lover did today:
I closed my eyes in carnal pleasure,
he feared I was dead, and ran away.   2338

DĀMODARAGUPTA

372

For treating bile the kiss is best,
for wind the pressure of her chest,
for phlegm it's ceaseless intercourse:
thus, for calming all three humours,
always to a girl recourse.   2340

373

A bed well made, a charming house,
a faithful and congenial spouse:
these a match can never prove
for a moment brief of secret love.   2342

DĀMODARAGUPTA

374

That strumpet is a box of bliss,
her cheek is pale with passion,
her pubic zone depilated is,
may all rascals get their ration.   2345

RANDĀNANDA

375

For one who comes
though not invited,
gets angry looks
but seats himself,
death is better
than any dinner.   2348

376

The letter *t* is always short
in rustic, servant, unchaste, cheat;
why it's doubled in priestly titles—
for this a harlot you must meet.   2352

377

Bribes, rewards and rental payments,
one should accept immediately;
the same is true of a share in wealth,
of stolen goods and poetry.
These six, not taken there and then,
may not be offered ever again.   2349

378

The priest keeps cows, but sells the milk,
and uses water for oblations
in the sacrificial fire.
He's also reputed to follow
the scriptures in sexual conduct,
but sleeps with menstruating whores,
and that in daylight too.   2353

379

Seeing a god made out of gold
the stones rejoice at their salvation
from being beaten, burnt and chiselled,
and bless the smith for his creation.   2354

SUVARṆAKĀRA IŚVARAVARMĀ

380

Fish prepared with oil and salt,
ginger, pepper, pomegranate peel,
with walnuts garnished, touched with saffron,
and served on a bed of cool, white rice:
the doer of this act of merit
is bound to go to paradise.   2357

381

The bed is small, its strings not tight,
the whoremaster talks incessantly,
worse luck, it's chill this winter night,
O what a load of misery!   2356

382

If I cut them off, what is
the point of living like an ox;
or like a bull by keeping them;
if I sit and stretch my legs,
people always laugh at me:
the size of my balls is a nuisance.   2355

RATNABHŪTI

383

He measures out rice
like Indra his diamonds,
and displays greens
like a barb from a bone,
but the sauce so spiced
that it burns the throat,
he serves most freely,
just like water.   2358

384

Even though one reaches eminence
by learning well the Vedas four,
the systems six, the fourteen skills,
and all the classic arts there are:
still one fails, if unaware
of the wheeling dealing here.   2359

385

Her waist is no more than a fist,
her belly is two arm's length round,
like swinging bells her two breasts list
towards the pelvis further down.
Her laughter's sound is like a horn,
her face can well inspire fear,
even so this courtesan
both repels and draws me near.   2360

386

Clad in a pair of white garments,
the girdle creased with three days' use,
his hair brushed upwards, legs and thighs
with razor scraped, there stands a man
looking out, by the temple bull,
for a quiet place to get some girl.   2361

387

Both good times and bad are certain
in this world for every creature.
An old man will be jilted by
young women, it's a part of nature.
In every clan there is a man
who gains great prosperity;
and if maids behave like menfolk can,
know that's the end of the family.   2362

388

He takes no meat or alcohol,
but drinks good people's blood;
though observing religious fasts,
he steals the temple food,
and that kept for cows and brahmins
while listening to the liturgy;
proud partner of these evil times,
whose friend can an official be?   2363

389

He asks you questions, tells strange tales,
scratches, feels inside his clothes,
looks at the sun and counts the days,
laughs excessively, swats mosquitoes,
goes out, quarrels with his workers,
drops a pitcher, puts out fire:
these are the goldsmith's dozen tricks
to distract you as he steals your gold.   2364-65

390

Do it, lover, while you may,
your youth is passing every day.
After death, who'll offer you
with funeral rites a sweet cunt too?   2366

391

May this whore give joy to you,
her gaze is candid, embrace soft,
and laughter graceful—never loud.
No more for her pursuit of pleasure,
she visits shrines and holy men;
but her breasts are large and firm,
of wits and panders she's still queen,
and all her lovers are good men.   2367

392

Harlots, too, look for salvation
and bliss with all intensity,
but, perhaps, in their devotions
just one blemish there could be:
and it is that, with lips perfumed
with scented wine and betel sections,
they kiss the mouths of holy priests
much defiled by benedictions.   2368

393

I have, my beauty, just one dollar,
it's in my belt for security;
I earned it with a lot of labour,
take half of it—be kind to me.   2370

394

With his cash, the harlot can
in any old and leprous man,
see a second god of love;
but moneyless, no better than
any old and leprous man
is a second god of love.   2369

KSHEMENDRA

395

In this chilly winter time,
may your cooking pots be full
with paste of lotus stem and root,
bright and smooth as elephant tusk,
with fritters rich in pepper,
and pieces of the shakuni fowl.   2371

396

She bears fresh nail marks on the thigh
but fears having them on other limbs;
her eyes are dull with sleep and red
with kisses, yet a flicker will
summon another paramour;
a wish-fulfilling vine for gallants,
this tart cannot be had without
many holy deeds of merit.   2373

397

The limbs are weak, it is futile
to stretch them out for an embrace;
the penis droops, to make it rise—
the mere effort is too hard to face
for the worn-out, flaccid flesh;
the girl's distressed, it is most awkward—
in making love, an old man's toil:
in thinking of it, what will be better—
to laugh a bit or weep a while?   2374

BHAṬṬA VRIDDHI

398

You are alert, can mind your limbs,
shake the head and move the feet,
answer questions, need less help,
and rice no more refuse to eat.
The fever's gone, and also thirst,
of chronic illness you are free
and looking, once again, alive,
it is a joy today to see.   2375

399

Grasping, like with meat a vulture,
guarding, like its hive the bee,
fierce like a sharp-clawed tigress,
venomous like a serpent, she
in turns and twists is like a fish,
in stealing things just like a mouse;
the harlot has so many aspects
for cheating clients in her house.   2377

400

Readings loud from holy books,
endless tales of piety,
talking much with womenfolk,
endearments for their progeny,
praise fictitious for their cooking,
their good fortune and competence,
blessings for their male relations,
some talk of one's experience,
and then a greeting once again:
in monks these are the merits main.   2378

401

Love purchased is like a medicine,
a labour, when to power due,
with one's spouse it's just mechanics:
it's something else which is love true.   2381

402

'Why is this food so salty dear?'
'Why don't you cook it on your own?'
'Hell! Don't you answer back like this!'
'To hell yourself! Your father too!'
'Damn you for your angry words!'
'You liar! Who gets angry more?'
With the couple always bickering,
can their torment ever end
and there be some joy?   2379

403

If, even though an utter fool,
you wish knowledgeable to appear
before a group of dull-wits, then
speak of eminent persons there,
take names of well-known authors,
display some books of quality,
some learned scholars vilify,
wave hands and laugh uproariously.   2383

404

For scholarship a reputation
if you wish to gain perforce,
even though to sacred learning
you have never had recourse:
then as your own, claim others' works,
stand proud as you recite some verse
with half-closed eyes, and be dramatic
while running down in language terse
Vyasa and the other lions
of literature in days gone by;
as for learned men at present,
challenge them, their skills decry.   2385

405

Friend, my husband has all the merits
which heroes, chiefs and princes do,
my life would have been worthwhile
if he were my lover too.   2387

406

My husband has these merits
which all young maids adore:
he sings and kisses like a bird,
in making love he's more
passionate than a rutting elephant.
A perfect moon? I have no word,
he's faultless but for one thing:
he is my wedded lord!   2386

407

Do not groan! O spinning wheel!
She sends us all in a spin
with a simple sidelong glance.
You, at least, are turned by hand.   2388

408

I hold the sacred thread, all pure,
and this solemn oath do swear:
than girls there's naught delightful more
nor greater trouble here.   2390

409

It pleases even when it's flowing,
even when the mind it shames;
this natural cleft delights the eye,
and shaven, shines in lovers' games;
it is the vagina, wondrous fair,
may all of you its blessings share.   2391

410

The sacred ground is marked for worship
with lotus flowers, but to hide
a cat's shit lying there, they use
the leaves kept for the ceremony.
It's like a fool, his sin to cleanse,
of sleeping with another's wife,
should call her 'mother' and thereby
aggravate it even more.   2392

411

For food forbidden, sick men hanker,
for money those in penury,
for hurting others, wicked people,
women for the joys of adultery.   2393

412

He curses not the moon, nor waits
for sweet words from a messenger;
burning sighs don't singe his heart,
his body does not waste away;
he sleeps embracing his own spouse,
one faithful and amenable.
Is it love? It's not, alas,
just the tiresome married state.   2398

413

Its friction makes the girls cry out,
young women emit squeals of joy;
the more mature, this rod ambrosial,
makes their deepest griefs forget;
it churns the oceanic depths
of old vaginas, like Mandara;
long live this tusk of Indra's elephant,
this mighty club, this prick of yours.   2401

414

'Monk, your cloak is rather loose.'
'It is a net for catching fish.'
'You eat fish?' 'With wine betimes.'
'You drink?' 'When with a courtesan.'
'You go to them?' 'I kick my enemies.'
'You have foes?' 'I burgle their homes.'
'You also steal?' 'Because I gamble.'
'You rogue!' 'I am a slave-girl's son.'   2402

415

'Someone else enjoys the pleasure
in being used, the pain our lot,'
the crone's breasts seem to say while reaching
down towards the other spot.   2406

22. Pen Pictures

416

Eager for home, the traveller goes
singing, laughing, dancing,
thinking of the girl in his heart,
not the ups and downs of the road.   2408

417

First they grunt like rumbling clouds
and slowly arch their bodies,
then, scraping with their hooves the earth,
pointing their horns straight ahead,
slowly, slowly, close they come
and, feet firm planted, strike furiously,
their curving tails uplifted:
these two big bulls afighting.   2424

418

Night is over, and the cat
gets up from beneath the oven,
yawns and twitches all its limbs
to shake the cinders out.   2407

419

The child covers its mouth and nose
with the hand, all fingers stretched out,
and loudly squeals:
my heart it steals.   2411

VALLABHADEVA

420

He takes a few uncertain steps
holding to the nurse's hand,
then, with the confidence of practice,
he comes crawling on all fours,
showing tiny buds of teeth.
Words cannot describe, O friend,
the pleasure given by one's child.   2414

BHAṬṬA JANĀRDANA

421

'Please, good mother, pity me,
a stranger who is tired out.
I'll pass the night in just a corner
of the porch outside your door
sleeping very quietly.'
Pleading thus, but quick rebuffed
by the housewife's sharp abuse,
the traveller picks up his possession,
a bundle no more than a fistful
of straw, and moves on again.   2416

RAVIDATTA

422

Hearing his mother say
'Your father's come!'
all at once the little boy
leaves his game with other children
and, dust covered, arms spread out,
comes shouting from afar and smiling,
to one who cannot but be blessed
by this love supreme.   2415

423

The donkey sniffs the odour, and
mouth agape, displaying teeth,
he runs braying loud behind
the fleeing she-ass, her kicks redoubling
his urge to copulate.
With organ taut he mounts her fast
but is bewildered and comes down,
his natural wish denied.   2422

ŚRI MAYŪRA

424

From the clouds the water streaming
at midnight in the palm forest,
the elephants stand with half-shut eyes,
their palm-leaf ears now motionless,
and listen to the falling rain,
their trunks reclining on their tusks.   2413

23. Verses of Flattery

425

'Why serve Krishna
who churned and hurt me,
and sleeps all day
upon my waves?
Better wait on someone
who understands, is kindly
and always wide awake.'
Thinking thus, and cognizant
of your fame, O king,
the sea of milk has here arrived
in the guise of snow to serve you.   2632

*

When the clouds were raining snow,
this verse, commixed with flattery,
addressed to Śrī Jainollābhadīn,
was made by Śrī Baka, that is me.   2633

426

Averse to engagement
even when summoned,
not showing openly
the play of its parts,
and unable to act
like a man upon you,
your enemy's army
is like a new bride.   2489

VIKAṬANIṬAMBĀ

427

It is stainless and strong,
pure, well tempered,
of noble lineage
and always sheathed.
Your sword wins hearts,
for it is like you.   2471

428

In the rich, generosity;
in the great, humility;
in well-born women, modesty;
on a person's tongue, poetry;
in elephants, ichor; in woods, a koel;
on buds, a bee; in bed a girl;
a nail mark on the beloved's cheek:
O king, all these are ornaments,
as you are of the world.   2622

429

Why ever talk of happenings
in other people's homes,
but with my southern, talkative,
nature I cannot be silent.
In every house, in markets,
in squares and drinking parties,
your darling madly circulates,
she is, sir, your fame.   2544

MĀTANGA DIVĀKARA

430

O king, your glory is adorned
by your mind, your mind by learning,
your learning by good policies,
your policies by valiant prowess,
your valour by your fame,
your fame by deeds, your deeds by brilliance
traditional in your family
which your birth itself adorns.   2577

431

Listen, king, in heaven, earth,
or in the nether world of serpents,
there never was or is or will be
any chief who can compare
in statecraft, glory, modesty,
in foes' destruction, love of art,
in piety and in fame with you.   2514

432

'Whose verse is this?' 'It's only mine.'
'Good, read it out again, sir poet.
But, friend, it has been used before!
Others have expressed this thought.'
The pain which such words cause to poets,
like axe strokes on their vine of hope,
O king, may your enemies suffer too.   2568

24. Verses of Counsel

433

Some are deer in tigers' garb,
some are tigers dressed as deer;
to place your trust in such reversals
is to invite trouble here.   2738

434

If you are unable to follow
the path of good men all the way,
pursue it even a little bit,
on that road one can't be lost.   2641

435

The greatest dharma is to do
good to others, well and true;
no greater wealth can ever be
than in one's work dexterity;
no pleasure is delightful more
than giving in a worthy cause;
and true salvation is to be
from every earthly craving free.   2642

436

The goddess of prosperity
will never go near one
who is too noble-minded,
too generous, bold and pious,
and proud of his own intellect:
she's scared of such a person.   2646

437

The lazy will not wealth attain,
nor the timid, or the proud,
or those who fear the people's clamour,
and folk who just wait all the time.   2647

438

For one whose self is ill-secured
even friends are enemies:
for weak digestions, even wholesome
food can sickness cause or death.   2653

439

'What will not, will never be,
what will, must come to pass for sure.'
For every care this remedy,
why not take and fret no more.   2662

440

Without harming others,
yielding to the wicked,
and giving up the right path,
what little one gets—
it is enough.   2660

441

In pain, look at a greater pain,
in pleasure, on some greater pleasure,
to grief and joy do not surrender—
both are your foes in equal measure.   2668

442

Look at the outcome
of constant practice:
even fools become
knowledgable, gradually,
mountains turn to powder,
termites consume a tree.   2679

443

Of family, friends and kinsmen,
of one's own mind and grit,
man discovers the reality
on the touchstone of calamity.   2688

444

An ant on the move can go
a hundred miles or more,
but an eagle, motionless,
will not progess
a single step for sure.   2686

445

The soft approach
is never respected,
the hard leads always
to enmity;
abjure both and follow
a middle policy.   2692

446

In all three worlds
there is no charm
to compare with this
for winning others:
friendliness and charity,
sweetness of speech, and
for each creature, sympathy.　　2694

447

From foes and fear and grief protecting,
your pleasures and your trust respecting,
who coined this word, this apophthegm
called 'friend' which is, in fact a gem.　　2700

448

Thinking that all comes from fate,
effort you should not disdain,
without pressing seeds of sesame,
who can oil from them obtain?　　2723

449

One who sits back, full of trust,
after making peace with enemies,
is like the man sleeping
on the branch of a tree
who will wake up on falling down.　　2756

450

A group with many leaders,
each one proud and clever,
and all wishing to be important,
is bound to be ruined.　　2724

451

By a foe, with respect treated,
you may another eliminate,
as you would a thorn
stuck in the foot
with one held in the hand.   2763

452

To those who live on Malaya's slope,
sandal is but firewood;
gems no more than rocks and stones
for denizens of the ocean's shore;
the residents of Kashmir, too,
have no respect for saffron:
distance lends great value, and
proximity breeds disdain.   2942

453

Replanting uprooted trees,
culling those in flower,
helping small ones grow,
and pruning those too tall or dense,
separating the intertwined,
placing thorny shrubs aside,
and nurturing those he plants:
a clever king, acting the gardener,
rules his realm for long.   2947

454

Better than a foolish brood
is a single child with merit:
darkness does one moon preclude,
a thousand stars can't do it.   2730

455

By mere touch can elephants kill,
by sniffs alone the serpents will,
sovereigns with a smile do slay,
and villains as they homage pay.   2752

456

Danger one should always dread,
as long as it is far away.
But once it is upon your head—
strike a blow as heroes may.   2755

457

The wise will not use
harsh methods, where
softer ones can work:
if bile is calmed
with sugar, why
use the bitter gourd?   2874

                                    ARGAṬA

458

With money one has many a friend,
and kinsmen too, one also can
on being acclaimed a sage depend,
one is then counted as a man.   2816

459

To consort with another's wife,
to hanker for another's wealth,
to insult teachers and elders,
neither gives happiness here
nor in afterlife.   2900

                                    RĀHULAKA

460

One whose repute
is not acclaimed
for death in war or victory,
for learning or for charity
or for great wealth:
his existence
has little difference
from that of an insect.   2901

VARĀHAMIHIRA

461

One who even guards a cent
from ever being wrongly spent,
as if a hoard of gold it were;
but will spending millions dare
when situations so demand,
and do it with an open hand—
the goddess of prosperity
will never leave one such as he.   2911

ŚRI HARSHA

25. On Dharma

462

This is the essence of dharma,
listen to it attentively:
do not do to others
what you would not like done to you.   2950

463

Kinsmen turn away and go
leaving the dead person's body
on the ground like a log of wood:
dharma alone does follow it.   2954

464

Earn that treasure, in having which
there is no fear of thief or king,
and which will always stay with you,
even after death.   2957

465

Straightforwardness and kindness,
self-restraint, control of the senses:
this is the common dharma of
all four castes, Manu has said.   2959

466

Truth is not just a word for the real,
nor falsehood for that which is unreal;
where lies the ultimate benefit
of creatures—that is real truth.   2969

467

In moving or in standing still,
in sleeping and in dreaming too,
whatever your actions be—
if not for the benefit of others,
they are but animal activity.   2970

468

The difference between recipients
unworthy or not of a gift
is as with cows and snakes:
with one grass turns into milk,
with the other milk into poison.   2975

469

Earned lawfully and gifted,
even a penny bears mighty fruit,
but not the thousands given
of wealth obtained illegally.   2976

470

They too must experience pain
when pricked even by a thorn,
yet such people savour flesh
of animals butchered with knives.   2982

471

For those who drink wine, kill a priest,
steal, or break a solemn vow,
atonement is possible, O king,
but none for one ungrateful.   2988

472

Non-violence, truth, compassion for
all creatures, self-restraint,
and charity within one's means:
this is the householder's dharma. 3010

473

In all man's actions
what needs discernment
is purity of intent:
the mistress is kissed with one,
the daughter with another. 2966

474

Rituals holy, sacred study,
doing penance, charity,
truth, forgiveness, solicitude,
and not coveting: virtue's road
with these eight, the scriptures say,
is paved to form the righteous way.
But, of these the first four go
to serve often an outward show.
The latter four can only be
in someone with true piety. 2997-98

475

In action, mind and speech,
to be devoid of malice
for all beings, and to show
them kindliness and charity:
this, the wise have said,
is true morality. 3047

476

Guard character with care,
wealth will come and go,
man is not lost by loss of money,
but without character he is dead.   3048

477

Knowledge is wealth in foreign lands,
common sense in times of trouble,
virtue is wealth in afterlife,
and good character everywhere.   3053

KSHEMENDRA

478

Just as when a garment's soiled,
it's so no matter where you sit,
character too, once it is spoiled
has nothing left for guarding it.   3049

26. *The Iron Age of Kali*

479

As the Age of Kali ends
all will be demons, who
in the shape of human beings,
eat other men, not in the flesh,
but by devouring their money.   3056

VYĀSA

480

This wicked Iron Age has taken
mankind into such condition
that wanting to cause injury
to the master and the friend
is a merit thought to be.   3058

481

By every dread disease afflicted,
to plunder by cut-throats subjected,
by kings oppressed, to famines bound,
the people now go round and round.   3064

482

The time is past when one's worth grew
with good and honest work;
now do not take the useless trouble
of acquiring merit;
instead, to get on with your life,
resort to shameless impudence.   3065

483

'What hope from that villain?'
'But he is good-hearted
and I have done a lot for him.'
'Forget it. Good is just a word
in ancient books. Today
people care only for money,
even a little bit of it.'   3066

484

In this Age of Kali, when dharma
has retired from this world;
truth and penance disappeared;
the earth is turning infertile,
the people cheats, the brahmins fools,
the rulers thoughtless and oppressive;
and sons hate fathers, wives fight husbands;
blessed are they who are dead.   3076

485

Moonlit nights they spend at brothels,
in ardent festivals of pleasure
amidst women with wine-scented mouths.
In daytime, as all-knowing ascetics,
since long engaged in sacred rituals,
ordained and fully enlightened,
these rascals cheat the world.   3077

486

'Where to, brother?' 'To the city.'
'For what?' 'In the hope of a job.'
'With whom?' 'The king.' 'But how?'
'On my merits.' 'And what are they?'
'Those of all decent people.'
'What use are they today!' 'What then?'
'Take to the forest. Haven't you heard?
Greedy villains are favoured now,
and jobs go to the scandalmongers.'   3072

27. The Power of Past Deeds

487

As among a thousand cows
the calf runs after its mother,
so too deeds done previously
always pursue the doer.

3081

488

Salute the gods? But even they
cannot escape relentless fate.
Salute that fate? But even it
bears fruit to deeds proportionate.
Then, if fruit depend on deeds,
are gods and fate of any avail?
Salutations to deeds on which
even fate cannot prevail.

3079

489

Such is the marvel in this world
of deeds done in a previous birth:
the undisciplined live long lives,
the servile have of wealth no dearth.

3084

490

Why be depressed in adverse times
and wonderstruck in prosperity?
It is by previous deeds decided,
whatever has to be will be.

3087

491

The fruit which deeds of people bear
are most uneven, it is seen:
some the palanquin do carry,
some ride upon the palanquin.   3092

492

Whatever man earns
with lifelong labour,
his heirs divide
when he is dead;
the evil he did
for greed of wealth
alone remains
that unfortunate's property.   3099

VYĀSA

493

Fruit come not from looks or family,
morals, learning or pure speech.
It is merit amassed from deeds
done by man in former lives
that bears fruit for him
in due time, like a tree.   3100

AŚVAGHOSHA

494

The man to whom
the gods award
defeat, his mind
they overturn:
he sees things
upside down.   3095

28. Fate

495

O the supreme ability
of fate which often marks
its scheme of distribution:
where merit stays, there is no money,
where money is, there stays no merit.   3108

ŚRI VYĀSA MUNĪ

496

As, in giving away a daughter,
one ensures the quality
of family, learning, prowess, age
and good character of the groom,
so does clever destiny
when it hands out poverty.   3109

497

Fate is the master
not just of men
but even of the gods.
Though Shiva's friend
is the god of wealth,
yet his garment
is animal skins.   3111

RAVIGUPTA

498

Something beyond one's wildest wish,
beyond even the poet's fancy,
hard to attain even in a dream,
yet fate bestows it in a trice.   3115

499

Base, impious, meritless,
fickle minded, harsh of speech,
if such a one great wealth enjoys,
is it his prowess, or his fate?   3116

VALLABHADEVA

500

When the sun eclipsed I see,
and elephants wild in fettered state,
and able men in poverty,
Then I realize the power of fate.   3125

501

Alas, the folly of fate!
In man it has created
a mine of limitless merits,
a jewel to adorn the earth,
yet made his existence
so very transitory.   3126

PHALGUHASTINI

502

A bald man's head was getting scorched
by the rays of the noonday sun.
Seeking shade, he stopped perchance
beneath a bilva tree, wherefrom
a great ripe fruit fell on his head
and cracked it with a loud report.
Disasters often happen just
where unlucky people chance to go.   3141

DIVIRADEVĀDITYA

503

Though tossed by angry winds of fate,
the sea, which is the noble heart,
will not transgress its proper limit,
that is the way of its waves.   3107

GOVINDARĀJA

504

In placing wish-fulfilling trees
on Mount Sumeru, whose celestial
denizens have no wishes left;
gems within the fathomless
waters of the mighty ocean;
and affluence with wicked villains;
the Creator has, in truth, blacked out
a bright lamp with a pot.   3135

PRAKĀŚAVARSHA

505

For serpents the Creator made
a diet of air, obtained with ease
without recourse to violence;
for beasts He laid young shoots and grass
to eat, and ground to sleep upon;
but for men, with wits to cross
the ocean of this worldly round,
were made such means of livelihood—
in securing which men's virtues
are, one and all, destroyed.   3139

                                    BHARTRIHARI

506

A snake, confined inside a basket,
lay hungry, coiled, all hope exhausted,
when, at night, a mouse crept in
through a hole that it had bored
and fell into the serpent's mouth.
Revived by its flesh, the snake
escaped by that very mouse-made hole.
So, be at ease, it's fate alone
which ensures the rise and fall of men.   3143

29. Times of Trouble

507

It is better to be born a tree
growing in some barren patch,
by fire of its bark denuded,
stunted, eaten up by worms,
than a supplicant to be.   3166

508

'Sit down! Stand up! Come here! Away!
Speak! Be silent!' Even so—
with supplicants who to them go,
gripped by hope, do rich men play.   3168

509

The ashen face, the voice choked up,
the trembling body, the perspiration:
these signs of one about to die
are the very same as of one
who has to make a supplication.   3172

510

Blessed are they who do not see
the break-up of their family,
their wives in love with other men,
their children caught in vice's den,
and their country cease to be.   3173

511

Moonlight, lutes and sandalwood,
beds and coaches, maidens nice,
cannot please a famished man:
all must start with a plate of rice.   3174

512

Forbear you did, but not forgive,
pleasures give up, but not in peace,
suffered chill winds, unbearable heat,
but without penitential spirit;
with every breath you thought of money,
night and day, but not of Shiva:
all the ascetic's deeds you've done,
but their fruit escape you.   3178

513

Living is like death
for one sick or exiled
or dependent on others
for daily bed and board;
death for him is rest.   3184

514

We were cut down by sharp-edged swords
of insult, scorn and humiliation;
burnt and branded through and through
by fierce flames of penury;
we even quaffed the venomous brew
of favours done by kinsmen; yet
we go on living. Is the god
of death so fast asleep?   3179

515

The cold gives me goose pimples,
like hair upon a bean pod.
The fire has gone out.
My lips are chapped with blowing,
and throat parched with sneezing.
I drown in a sea of worry.
Sleep left me like a lover scorned
and fled far away.
And night, like well-invested wealth,
goes on and on forever.   3181

MĀTRIGUPTA

516

When their money's gone, the base
live as beggars, cheats and bandits;
for the good, whom family honour keeps
silent, there is no more life.   3182

KSHEMENDRA

517

For lack of money, every day
worrying over rice and oil,
greens, butter, salt and firewood,
dulls the minds of even the wise.   3188

518

A golden beast is just impossible,
yet Rama wanted such a deer;
often the mind turns contrary
when disaster is drawing near.   3189

519

No rice inside the pot,
the family faint and famished;
no lamp to burn at night;
all facilities plunged in darkness;
no well-wishers at the door,
the festivities suspended;
alas this house has turned
as painful as a prison.   3192

520

In my home the mouse has turned
as minuscule as a mosquitoe,
the cat has shrunk to mouse's size,
the dog is no more than a cat.
What to say of other people,
my wife is worn out, like a dog;
and, witness to the dying babies,
the oven hides in spider webs,
the cricket's hum its mournful cry.   3197

30. On Being a Servant

521

Hug a tiger with gaping jaws,
kiss a serpent's hissing mouth,
for men to serve kings is no better:
it is like licking a razor's edge.   3225

522

The master laughs, and so does he;
the master weeps, he wails aloud;
the master runs, he girds his waist
and sprints, sweating profusely;
the master censures some unblemished
merit, he condemns it:
the servant, bought for a bit of money,
dances to his master's tune.   3232

DHARMAKIRTI

523

Your Majesty's ears I filled
with words devoid of meaning;
you too did the same with me,
the words even more inane.
Thus we both have passed our time
deceiving one another.
My strength now fades, I am defeated,
you win, you are the king.   3234

KIŚORAKA

524

It's always hard to find a master,
forgiving and generous, who
respects and values merit;
to find a loyal, honest, clever
servant, sir, is difficult too.   3228

ŚRI HARSHADEVA AND HIS SERVANT

525

The servant is deprived of both
his comfort and his dignity;
of that for which he money seeks,
he poorer tends to be.   3211

526

He does not care
if you're stopped at the door;
takes no notice
when you manage to meet him;
blinks like an elephant
at your presentation;
pretends to agree
and, after you leave,
runs you down.
At the smallest fault
a very death,
if you serve such a master,
what is wrong
with the ghouls of the desert?   3238

KSHEMENDRA

31. Cravings

527

Mounted on the chariot of desire,
drawn by steeds which are the senses,
all the world goes round and round,
urged on by craving, the charioteer.   3241

528

The face is covered with wrinkles,
the head has gone all grey,
the limbs are slack and feeble,
only cravings youthful stay.   3242

529

The teeth have gone, the hair turned grey,
speech chokes, one falters on the way,
but craving, like a faithful wife,
will not the ageing carcass leave—
though it is set to part with life.   3254

530

One with a hundred wants a thousand,
the thousand-owner to make a million,
the millionaire to be a king,
the king to be an emperor,
the emperor a god, and he
the lord of heaven, and even then
to have some still higher position—
there is no end to craving.   3255-56

531

Craving is a crafty whore
who deludes everyone,
robbing helpless fools
of the wealth of peace.
With Kama, sly and crooked rogue,
and sparkling liquid sidelong glances
of false love, she is ever adept
in letting loose disaster.   3263

KSHEMENDRA

532

Love is like milk: it is boiled
and cream is taken out,
then it is churned to make butter
and boiled again for ghee.
Loving seems to get attached
to some kind of calamity.   3259

SUBHADRĀ

533

In many inaccessible lands
I knocked about, but gained nothing.
With anxious and tormented mind,
setting aside the family's honour,
I spent my youth in fruitless work
of servants, but to no avail.
O craving, what more do you wish,
for that too I am ready.   3262

534

Craving, like a wanton woman,
urges men to deeds forbidden
but shame protects them from all sins
like a second mother.   3245

535

O craving, you too crave to dwell
in three particular places—
in ailing people and the childless
and in those bowed down with age.   3248

32. Transience

536

Wealth is pleasing, it is true,
pretty girls delightful too,
but life, like sidelong looks and sly
of wanton women, just flits by.

3266

537

Death is certain for the born.
Birth is certain for the dead.
Therefore you should not lament
for what is unavoidable.

3269

538

Those who wake to the sound of music
and sweet song, and orphans, who
on others for their food depend:
death takes equally the two.

3273

539

The rich man's wealth is that alone
which he spends or gives away;
with the rest, when he is gone,
and with his wives, will others play.

3283

540

Drifting in the sea's expanse,
as two logs will meet by chance,
and having met, will part perforce—
such is creatures' intercourse.

3287

541

Death is certain for all creatures,
it's certain life is transitory,
who indeed can know today
whose tomorrow's dawn will be?   3284

542

Mortals, why are you afraid
of death? It will not spare
the fearful. Only the unborn
it does not take—so try
never to be born again.   3295

543

In childhood bound in ignorance,
drunk in youth with arrogance,
in old age all the limbs afflicted—
when can one be really well?   3302

ŚRI BAKA

544

Today it is childhood,
soon the glory of youth,
then senescence. When the body
itself keeps changing,
how can one rely
on things outside it.   3304

VĀLMIKI MUNI

545

Enchanting girls, congenial friends,
good kinsmen, sweetly speaking servants,
all facilities, horses, elephants:
but once your eyes are closed,
not a whit of this remains.   3318

ŚRI VIKRAMĀDITYA

546

'I am here, this is my father,
this my mother, spouse and field,
my family, children, friends and foes,
my wealth and house, my kin and siblings.'
On the bed which is this world,
long asleep in ignorance,
O mind deluded, you do see
many dreams like this.   3321

KRISHNA MIŚRA

547

Property is like waves on water,
youth lasts for two days, perhaps three,
life flits by like autumn clouds,
what use is wealth? Do charity!   3316

548

Learned ones! Attend on God!
Cling not to painful scriptural study,
for in this and the other worlds
Shiva is the only saviour.
When death's unceasing, dreadful danger
comes on you by fate's decree,
what will you gain from grammar, logic
or even resort to poetry?   3322

SRIMAD RĀKJĀNAKA LAULAKA

549

In summer, ice and sandal paste,
Chinese silk and moonlight;
in winter, deerswool shawls, and girls
with saffron-tinted breasts embraced;
at night the sound of flutes, and songs
of courtesans, and in the day
fine assemblies: all of this
done for an ungrateful body.
It is handsome, but will it last?   3323

KSHEMENDRA

550

This treasure serves the fourfold ends,
it's hard to get and lasts a moment,
now having it, if you do not
think about your real benefit,
who knows if you will ever have
this human form again.   3313

BODHISATTVA

551

Not one moment of this life
can be ever had again
even for a million sovereigns.
One who spends it to no purpose—
salute that beast in human form.

3307

33. Derision of Lust

552

Even the mighty ocean's surge,
propelled by fierce and violent winds,
it is possible to restrain—
but not the infatuated mind.   3333

ŚRI VYĀSA MUNI

553

If that which is within the body
were to be outside it,
people would be brandishing
sticks to ward off dogs and crows.   3334

554

The hunter Kama has spread out
the nets you here discern—
it's only by their power
that hell fires burn.   3337

555

It's like a slit upon the bloated
belly of a frog turned upside down:
who but a maggot would be drawn
to this slimy sore?   3341

556

This loathsome ulcer
soiled with faeces and sweat,
flowing urine and blood,
has blinded all the world.   3342

557

Thinking about sense-objects
brings you close to them;
from closeness springs desire
which, thwarted, turns to anger.
From anger comes delusion,
confusing the memory;
memory's loss destroys the mind,
and with that man is lost.   3344-45

VYĀSA MUNI

558

In this life, so full of pain,
there is no greater misery—
your longings cannot be fulfilled,
nor are you from longings free.   3350

559

Desire is never stilled
by its satisfaction.
The sacred fire burns more brightly
with every new oblation.   3352

560

Born, he takes away your wife,
growing, takes away your wealth,
in dying, takes away your life,
there is no enemy like the son.   3367

ŚRI VYĀSA MUNI

561

Their words are full of honey,
their hearts have only poison:
so, drink from the lips of women,
but press and squeeze their breasts.   3380

KĀLIDĀSA AND MĀGHA

562

A handsome young woman,
sitting or standing,
in sleep reclining,
the face turned away,
beautifully dressed
or not at all, when seen
by weak-minded men
will always attract them
even through she
is just in a picture.   3382

563

A scrawny cur,
one-eyed and lame,
with bitten ears
and tattered tail,
old and starving,
the foot stuck in a
a broken potsherd,
covered with sores
exuding pus
and slimy maggots:
yet this dog
pursues a bitch—
Kama maddens
even him.   3390

564

Even though they may endure for long,
sensual pleasures must inevitably fade away.
What difference does it make if people
will not give them up willingly?
If they cease on their own, it grieves the heart
immeasurably; but if they are renounced
it gives one the infinite happiness of peace.   3386

JAYĀDITYA

34. Regrets

565

All my life has slipped away
just in nursing aspirations,
even now I have done nothing
by good men worth remembering.   3393

566

To pleasures, now farewell,
goodbye to talk of love,
alas, I am so very old,
those bright-eyed girls just look through me.   3395

567

My youth went by in a whirl
of bargains of beauty in markets of love;
now wrinkles make a thousand patterns
on the canvas of my body;
only the mind, discarding shame,
keeps ever growing young.   3397

568

We did not enjoy pleasures,
we were consumed by them;
we did not observe austerity,
it branded us instead;
time did not pass,
it is we who are passing;
cravings do not wear away,
only we are worn out.   3396

569

I never acquired learning,
well-honed and suitable
for silencing disputants.
I did not spread my fame
to the sky with the sword,
piercing heads of war-elephants.
Nor did I in moonlight drink
nectar from the tender lips
of a pretty girl.
Alas, my youth passed uselessly,
like a lamp burning
in an empty house.

3400

35. Aspiration

570

Lord, surrendering to you all
my works of body, mind and speech,
will I ever freedom gain
from contradictions and become
myself a part of you?   3402

571

Lord, when will I stand before you
with the lamp of understanding
which burns the wick of worldliness
steeped in the oil of sin?   3403

572

A holy rosary in my hands,
at my throat the sacred beads,
auspicious ash upon my body,
my hair a tawny matted coil,
a piece of bark around my shoulders:
thus may I live in tranquility
at a hermitage, beneath a tree.
What more? And may the name of Shambhu
in my ears forever be.   3411

573

Alone, at peace, of longings free,
my hands the cup, my clothes the sky,
able to renounce the world,
when will I, O Shambhu, be?   3404

574

The bliss unique of serving you,
is a tree-filled garden's shade
for a wanderer in the desert;
a well of ice-cold water for
one fleeing from a forest fire;
nectar from a brew of poison,
and one's self rescued from madness:
Shankara, when will I attain it
and overcome this separation?   3414

VĀKPATI, SON OF ŚRI HARSHADEVA

575

By the side of the river
which cleanses all sin,
with breezes blowing
and water at hand,
living in a hut
and wearing a rag,
I have no more relish
for this transient body.   3422

576

Maidens are no better than
poison for an aged man,
as food is poison for a person
who is suffering indigestion,
and the building of a house
for one as penniless as a mouse:
it is the same for learning, got
without having been truly taught.   3430

577

The man who eats
what he has earned
by his prowess and skill
truly eats,
for even dogs
eat what they get
by wagging their tails.   3432

578

Logic is inconclusive.
The scriptures differ.
There is no sage
whose word can be final.
The root of dharma
is hidden and secret.
The way by which
the great have gone—
that is the path.   3437

DINNĀGA

579

Those driven by money
have no friend or kin;
by carnal lust,
no fear or shame;
by search of knowledge,
no sleep or comfort;
by pangs of hunger,
no grace or lustre.   3441

580

None torment the body
like pangs of hunger;
nothing sucks it dry
as does worry;
nothing ornaments it
more than learning;
and nothing nourishes it
like a livelihood.   3442

581

O mind, you are so restless!
You plunge into the nether world
and traverse the firmament,
wandering in all directions.
Yet, though you course through
other regions and lands,
you do not touch the self within,
where you would find repose.   3447

ARGAṬA

582

Some act humble out of fear,
some out of greed
while seeking wealth,
others covet the fame of virtue.
No one in the world is good
purely out of goodness.   3449

CHANDRAGOPIN

583

It's greed or conceit, fear or shame,
which makes men modest, generally;
the modesty of heart which comes
from detachment is a rarity.   3450

BHAṬṬA ŚRIDATTA

584

What is the use of empty talk?
There are always two recourses
for men in this world:
handsome young women
weighed down by their breasts
and ardent with passion—
their wildness, or the wilderness.   3453

BHAṬṬA UDBHAṬA

585

The moon turned pale in daylight;
a beautiful woman past her youth;
a lake bereft of lotus flowers;
the handsome visage of a fool;
a skinflint master; a good man out of luck;
and a villain in royal favour:
these seven rankle
like barbs in my heart.   3458

BHAṬṬA VRIDDHI

586

Who, on attaining affluence,
does not succumb to arrogance?
When given up to pleasures, who
can to troubles bid adieu?
Who has never jilted been
by women on this earthly scene?
Who escapes death's fearful sting?
And who is the favourite of the king?
Which beggar ever gets respect?
Which man is there who can expect,
when fallen in a villain's snare,
to go home safe, without a care?   3470

FROM *PANCHATANTRA*

587

We are here content with rags,
and you with your great affluence.
The satisfaction is the same,
it has no special difference.
Man becomes a pauper
when his hankerings increase;
no one is rich or penniless
when the mind is at peace.   3475

588

O Lord, in serving you,
there is no checking at the door,
no question of a proper time,
no indignity or fear of villains,
no feeling small or a failure.
Even so, in every way,
we still keep serving other men.   3482

                          MADHUSŪDANA

589

You've stopped eating, turned away
from all that the senses seek;
with eyes fixed on your nose-tip
and mind immersed in concentration,
you are silent, as if the whole
world seems to you a void.
Tell me, friend, have you become
a yogini, or are you in love?   3485

37. Prayers

590

With almsgiving and pilgrimage,
penance and fire ceremony,
whatever will a person do
who keeps within his heart the Lord,
Hari, abode of felicity.   3486

591

In illness, the Lord
is the remedy supreme,
in darkness, the lamp,
in quandaries, the pathway,
the guard in dangers,
in troubles, the friend,
and in the deep ocean
of sorrow, the ship.   3494

ŚRĪ VIKRAMĀDITYA

592

I always remember
the divine child sleeping
on a leaf of the fig tree,
holding with his rosy hands
the rosebud of his little foot
within the rose, his mouth.   3499

593

O Master, in your kindness
give ear to the pleas
of this wretch who has no entry
and weeps outside your door.   3501

ARCHITADEVA

594

No one is more afflicted than I,
no one more merciful than you:
our coming together is well matched,
Lord, how can you not save me?   3503

595

If I am not a mighty sinner,
were I not deluged by fear
and cemented to the senses,
what need have I to seek refuge?   3505

BHAṬṬA SUNANDANA

596

As determined by my deeds,
in every form that I am born,
in each of them may my devotion
to you, Hrishikeśa, steadfast be.   3508

597

Lord, I did not think of you,
exalt and praise you, sing your deeds,
I did not worship you devoutly
even with a blade of grass;
yet I seek your sanctuary,
be merciful to me.   3514

BHĀGAVATA ŚANKHA

598

Even when the distinction
disappears, O Lord,
I am yours, you are not mine:
the wave is of the ocean,
not the ocean of the wave.   3520

ŚANKARĀCHĀRYA

599

By ignorance blinded, friendless,
possessed by demons of the senses,
cast by inner ogres into
the depths of dark delusion's well,
home to all misfortunes, lost,
I weep and seek refuge in you,
do not abandon me, great god,
I am afraid, assure me.   3522

600

I am in distress, miserable
at all times, in every state,
I have surrendered to you, Lord,
save me, who seeks your sanctuary.   3527

The Poets

The poets to whom individual verses have been ascribed are listed below in alphabetical order, with brief details where available. As some of the listed names also figure in these details, they have been marked there with an asterisk for cross-reference.

The chronological and other details given in this list are sparse and not known with finality in many cases. In almost a quarter of them we know only the poet's name, which too would have been lost but for the ascription.

In several cases poets are named with titles or honorifics. Though fully reflected in the translation, these have been left out from the list to facilitate reference. The most common honorific excluded here is bhaṭṭa, a respectful term for a learned person. Others are muni, a sage; bhadanta, a Buddhist elder; rājaputra, a prince; and śrimad or śri, a prefix used with names of eminent people. The title rājānaka was used in ancient Kashmir for officials of rank. Some others are explained in the endnotes.

Amaruka Reputed author of *Amaruśataka*, the famous collection of love poems dated c. seventh century CE. The name is also spelt Amaru.

Amritadatta Contemporary of the Kashmiri potentate Shahabuddin, c. 1352. In some entries he is titled bhāgavata, which indicates a devotee of the god Vishnu.

Amritavardhana Has the title bhāgavata, but no other detail is available.

Ānandavardhana Leading poet and thinker under King Avantivarman of ninth-century CE Kashmir. Author of *Dhvanyāloka*, which proposes the doctrine of dhvani or suggestion in poetry.

Architadeva Some mss. give the name as Achintadeva, and the title bhāgavata, indicating a devotee of the god Vishnu. There is no further information.

Argaṭa He is also cited in an eleventh-century commentary on the work of Rudraṭa,* but only the name is known.

Ārogya A Buddhist monk known only by name.

Aśvaghosha Buddhist philosopher and writer dated to the first century CE. His major work is the biographical poem *Buddhacharita*.

Avantivarman King of Kashmir (855–84 CE).

Baka A poet contemporary of the fifteenth-century Kashmiri king Zainu'l Abidin. Also mentioned in the continued *Rājataringini* of Śrivara.

Bāṇa Famous Sanskrit stylist. Court poet of King Harsha of seventh-century CE Kannauj, and author of the royal biography *Harshacharita* and the novel *Kādambari*.

Bhallaṭa A poet contemporary of King Śamkaravarman of Kashmir (883–902 CE) and the author of a sataka or century of verse epigrams.

Bhāmaha Author of the eighth-century CE work from Kashmir on poetics *Kāvyālamkāra*, which is the earliest extant text on the subject after Bharata's *Nātyaśastra*.

Bhāravi Author of the epic poem *Kirātārjunīya*, dated to the sixth-century CE Pallava empire. Lauded by later critics and cited, along with Kālidāsa,* in the 634 CE Aihole inscription.

Bhartrihari Reputed author of the well-known *Śatakatrayam*, the three centuries of verse epigrams on policy (*niti*), pleasure (*śringāra*) and renunciation (*vairāgya*). Sometimes identified with the c. sixth–seventh century CE grammarian of the same name. A legend has him as the half-brother and predecessor of the celebrated king Vikramaditya of Ujjain.

Bhartrisvāmin Identified with the seventh-century CE poet Bhaṭṭi, whose epic poem *Rāvanavadha*, apart from retelling the *Rāmāyana* also illustrates the poetics of Bhāmaha.* Translated into Javanese, this work helped spread the Rama story in South-East Asia.

Bhāsa Dramatist praised by famous later writers including Kālidāsa* and Bāṇa.* Dated usually to first–second century CE. *Svapnavāsavadattā* is the best known of the plays ascribed to him.

Bhaśchu Sometimes identified with the names Bharchu and Bharvu, which occur in other anthologies.

Bhaṭṭārka Only the name is known.

Bījaka Only the name is known.

Bilhaṇa Author of *Vikramānkadeva Charita*, the history of a Chālukya king of Kalyāṇa in Karnataka, and *Chaurapanchaśikā*, a collection of love poems. Placed in eleventh–twelfth century Kashmir.

Bodhaka Only the name is known.

Bodhisattva Only the name is known.

Brahmayaśasvāmi Only the name is known.

Chandaka Also written as 'Chandraka'. He is mentioned by the writers Kshemendra* and Kalhaṇa,* so would have lived before the eleventh century.

Chandragopin Identified with a grammarian of this name.

Chiāka Only the name is known.

Chūlitaka Only the name is known.

Dāmodaragupta Minister of the eighth-century CE king Jayāpīḍa of Kashmir and author of *Kuttanīmata*, a novel in verse about the life of courtesans.

Dhairyamitra Only the name is known.

Dharmakīrti Celebrated Buddhist philosopher-logician dated to the seventh century CE.

Dhīranāga Author of the play *Kundamālā*. The name is also spelt Vīranāga or Dinnāga in some mss.

Dinnāga Eminent Buddhist philosopher, epistemologist and author, usually placed in fifth-century CE Kalinga (modern Orissa).

Dīpaka Author of the romance *Vinayavati*. Quoted in various anthologies.

Diviradevāditya Also mentioned as Devāditya in some mss, but only the name is known.

Govindarāja Only the name is known.

Govindasvāmi His name features in other anthologies too. In one he is shown as the joint author of a verse with Vikatanitambā.*

Harigaṇa Only the name is known.

Harsha There are two poets of this name: (1) King Harsha of Kannauj (606–46 CE), author of the plays *Ratnāvali*, *Nāgānanda* and *Priyadarśikā*, and patron of Bāṇa* and other poets. Some of his verses are sourced in the endnotes. (2) The twelfth-century author of the epic *Naishadhīya Charita*.

Harshadatta Only the name is known.

Indulekhā Only the name of this poetess is known.

Īśvaravarman Only the name is known.

Jalhaṇa Kashmiri poet, author of *Somapālavilāsa*. Was an official at Rājapuri, identified with modern Rajauri.

Janārdana Only the name is known.

Jayāditya Joint author with Vāmana of the well-known grammatical treatise *Kāśikā Vritti*.

Jayamādhava A poet only known through some anthologies.

Jayavardhana This poet figures in several anthologies, one of which describes him as a Kashmiri.

Jīvaka Only the name is known.

Kalhaṇa Author of *Rājataringini*, the celebrated verse history of Kashmir, where he lived in the twelfth century.

Kālidāsa Outstanding poet and dramatist of classical Sanskrit. Often placed at the imperial Gupta court c. fifth century CE. His verses are sourced in the endnotes.

Kallaṭa Author of *Spandasarvasva*, a commentary on the work of his teacher Vasugupta, the Shaiva philosopher. Mentioned by Kalhaṇa* among scholar contemporaries of King Avantivarman in ninth-century CE Kashmir.

Kamalāyudha A teacher of the better-known Vākpatirāja* who praises him as such in his poetic work of the seventh century CE, *Gaudavaho*.

Kaviputras Two poets who wrote under a joint name. Perhaps the subjects of a laudatory reference in Kālidāsa's *Mālavikāgnimitra*.

Kayyaṭa There are two Kashmiri writers with this name: (1) The author of a well-known treatise on grammar, *Bhāshyapradīpa*, dated to c. ninth century CE; (2) A tenth-century commentator on the *Deviśataka* of Ānandavardhana,* who was also the grandson of Vallabhadeva,* (but not the anthologist).

Kiśoraka Also quoted in other anthologies, but only the name is known.

Krishna Miśra Author of the twelfth-century play *Prabodhachandrodaya*.

Kshemendra Well-known poet, critic and polymath from eleventh-century Kashmir. Some of his verses are sourced in the endnotes.

Kumāra It has been suggested that this is the same as the blind poet Kumāradāsa, author of the seventh-century CE epic poem *Jānakiharaṇa*, much lauded by later critics.

Laulaka Sometimes identified as the grandfather of Jonarāja, a contemporary of King Zainu'l Abidin of Kashmir and author of the historical work *Rājāvali*.

Madhusūdana   Only the name is known.

Māgha Author of the sixth–seventh century CE epic poem *Śiśupālavadha*, much praised by later critics.

Mahāmanushya A poet cited in some anthologies, in one of which he is described as from Kashmir.

Mangalavatsa Only the name is known.

Mātanga Divākara Poet at the court of King Harsha of seventh-century CE Kannauj. Cited by the later critic Rājaśekhara* as a peer of Bāṇa.*

Mātrigupta A poet in Kashmir, mentioned by Kalhaṇa* and quoted by Kshemendra.*

Mātrisheṇa Only the name is known.

Maya Only the name is known.

Mayūra Father-in-law of Bāṇa,* and author of the poem *Sūryaśataka*.

Morikā A poetess known only from some anthologies.

Muktāpīḍa King of Kashmir c. 594 CE.

Muktikoshthaka Only the name is known.

Nagnajita The same name is mentioned by the astronomer Varāhamihira as an authority on statuary.

Nārāyaṇa Author of the celebrated seventh-century CE epic poem *Veṇīsamhāra*.

Narendra Only the name is known.

Nidrādaridra He is also cited in other anthologies, but nothing is known beyond the name.

Paribhūta Only the name is known.

Parpaṭi Only the name is known.

Phalguhastini This poetess is known only by name through two entries in the anthology.

Prabhākarananda Only the name is known.

Prakāśadatta Nothing known beyond the name.

Prakāśavarsha Has twenty-seven entries in the full anthology, but little is known about him. The c. ninth-century commentator Vallabhadeva* mentions him as his teacher, and he also features in other anthologies.

Pulina Only the name is known.

Puṇya Nothing known beyond the name.

Rāhulaka A poet also quoted in other anthologies, but only the name is known.

Rājaśekhara Well-known critic, poet and dramatist from tenth-century Kannauj, often quoted in anthologies. Author of the plays *Karpūramanjarī* and *Viddhasālabhanjikā*, the verse *Bālarāmāyana*, and *Kāvya Mimāmsā*, a treatise on poetics.

Randānanda Only the name is known.

Ratnabhūti Only the name is known.

Ratnamitra Only the name is known.

Ravidatta A poet quoted in several anthologies, but only the name is known.

Ravigupta Buddhist philosopher of eighth century CE, quoted in various anthologies. Author of *Chandraprabhā-vijaya Kāvya* and other works.

Rudraṭa Author of a treatise on poetics, *Kāvyālamkāra*, dated c. tenth century. Not to be confused with Bhāmaha.*

Śankarāchārya The great Vedanta philosopher usually dated to the eighth century CE, and author of some well-known devotional poetry.

Śankha Only the name is known. The title indicates a devotee of the god Vishnu.

Śankuka Mentioned in *Rājataringini* of Kalhaṇa* as the author of an epic poem, *Bhuvanābhyudaya*, and contemporary of King Ajitapīḍa of Kashmir (c. 813 CE).

Śaśivardhana Perhaps an associate of King Kalaśaka of Kashmir (1080–88 CE). One verse in the present anthology is ascribed jointly to both.

Śilā Bhaṭṭārikā Ninth-century CE poetess known only through anthologies.

Śrīdatta Only the name is known.

Subhadrā A poetess lauded by Rajaśekhara* in another anthology.

Śūdraka Author of the play *Mricchakaṭika*, well known in English translation as *The Little Clay Cart*. Dated to c. second–third century CE.

Śuga The titles indicate a high official, of whom only the name is known.

Sunandana Only the name is known.

Sūra Well-known Buddhist poet of c. fourth century CE. Author of the *Jātakamālā*, which was later translated into Chinese and Tibetan. Also known as Ārya Śūra.

Śūravarman Only the name is known.

Tathāgatendra Simha Only the name is known.

Trivikrama Author of the prose–verse narrative *Nalachampu*, also quoted by Kshemendra.*

Uchyamānānanda Only the name is known.

Udaya Only the name is known from the single entry in the anthology. The title upādhyāya indicates a teacher.

Udbhaṭa Poet and critic at the court of King Jayapīḍa of Kashmir (779–813 CE). Author of *Kāvyālamkāra Samgraha*, a treatise on poetics.

Vākpati Author of the Prakrit epic *Gaudavaho*, but the reference here to being the son of Harsha makes the identification problematic.

Vallabhadeva There are two writers with this name from Kashmir: a ninth-century CE commentator on the *Siśupālavadha* of Māgha,* and the fifteenth-century compiler of the present anthology. The latter has shown twenty-two entries under this name.

Vālmiki Known in tradition as the ādi kavi or the first poet, and the author of the *Rāmāyana*. This epic poem is ascribed to 400–200 BCE.

Varāhamihira Well-known sixth-century CE astronomer, whose verses are also quoted in anthologies.

Vararuchi A poet and grammarian cited in some anthologies as the author of *Kanthābharaṇam*.

Vibhūtibala The name alone is known from a single entry in the anthology.

Vidyādhipati This name has been identified as a title of Ratnākara, a poet at the court of King Avantivarman of Kashmir (855–84 CE), and the author of the epic *Haravijaya*, who is mentioned in *Rājataringini* of Kahaṇa.*

Vijjākā Sanskrit poetess known only from various anthologies. References in her verses place her between 650 and 850 CE. Also known as Vidyā.

Vikaṭanitambā Ninth-century CE poetess, acclaimed by the later critic Rajaśekhara.*

Vikramāditya Possibly associated with the better-known Kashmiri poet Mentha, with whom he is shown as the co-author of some verses in other anthologies. Mentioned in *Rājataringini* of Kalhaṇa.

Viśākhadeva Identified with Viśākhadatta, author of the c. eighth-century CE play *Mudrārākshasa*.

Viṭa Vritta The name alone is known from a single entry in the anthology.

Vriddhi Also mentioned as Śaka Vriddhi, which may be an indicator of his ethnic background.

Vrishnigupta Only the name is known.

Vyāghragaṇa Only the name is known.

Vyāsa The traditional author of the *Mahābhārata*. The kernel of this long epic poem is believed to have been composed c. fifth century BCE.

Notes

Introduction

1   Among the better known are *Subhāshitaratnakosha* of Vidyākara (Bengal, c. eleventh century); *Saduktikarṇāmrita* of Śridharadāsa (Bengal, 1205); *Sūktimuktāvali* of Jalhaṇa (Deccan, 1258); and *Paddhati* of Śārṇgadhara (Rajasthan, 1363), apart from the work discussed here. A modern compilation in the same tradition is *Subhāshita-ratnabhāndāgāra* of N.R. Acharya (Mumbai, 1952). Only the first mentioned of these anthologies has an English translation (by D.H.H. Ingalls, Harvard Oriental Series, vol. 44).

2   The best known of these are the *Śatakas* of Bhartrihari and Amaruka, both perhaps c. seventh century. The first has the themes of *niti* (policy), *śringāra* (pleasure) and *vairāgya* (renunciation), while the second has only erotic poems. *Padyāvali* of Rupa Gosvāmin, sixteenth century, is a collection of devotional verses.

3   See 1 above. A fuller list of both types is given in S. Bhattacharji's article on anthologies in *Glimpses of Sanskrit Literature*, ed. A.N.D. Haksar, New Delhi, 1995.

4   M. Winternitz, *History of Indian Literature*, vol. 3, tr. S. Jha, Delhi, 1963; A.B. Keith, *A History of Sanskrit Literature*, Oxford University Press, 1920. Hereafter referred to as Winternitz and Keith.

5   Winternitz.

6   P. Peterson, notes to his edition of *Subhāshitāvali*, mentioned in the Introduction.

7   Winternitz. Keith. A.K. Warder, *Indian Kāvya Literature*, vols. 2–7, Delhi 1990–2004. J. Brough, *Poems from the Sanskrit*, London, 1968.

8   For example v. 1253 in the original, the first line of which reads in Sanskrit: *sa me samāsamo māso sā me māsasamā samā*. This describes the lover's feelings when the beloved is absent

or present. An English rendering would be 'a month is like a year for me, a year is like a month', but the impact, which derives from the alliterative use of only two consonants in the line, in words meaning month (*māsa*) and year (*samā*), is lost in translation.

9 D.H.H. Ingalls, *Sanskrit Poetry*, Harvard University Press, 1965.

10 *Subhāshitaratnakosha*, ed. D.D. Kosambi and V.V. Gokhale, Harvard Oriental Series, vol. 42, Harvard University Press, 1957.

Anthology

Several deities from the Hindu pantheon are mentioned in the verses. Sharada is another name for Sarasvati, goddess of learning, speech and the arts, with an important shrine in Kashmir. The trinity of Brahma, Vishnu and Shiva, the great gods associated with creation, preservation and dissolution, is well known. The second, also called Hari, is invoked in his various incarnations, notably as Krishna, whose childhood with his foster-mother Yashodā, was extolled with deep devotion. The other incarnations of Vishnu described here are as the divine boar, who recued the earth from the deluge, and the great tortoise, on whose back was placed the mountain used by the gods and the demons to churn the ocean of milk. Lakshmi, the goddess of prosperity, is Vishnu's consort and rests with him on a serpent couch in the ocean. Shiva is often addressed here as Shambhu, giver of peace and happiness. Guha, here depicted as an artless infant, is his son. So is Ganapati, the elephant-headed god who removes obstacles. Indra or Shakra is the king of heaven. Manmatha and Madana are other names for Kama, god of love and symbol of desire. Hrishikeśa is an epithet of Vishnu and Krishna.

Many of the notes on the numbered individual verses refer to their sources as known to present scholarship. Those occuring more frequently in this selection are indicated by abbreviations, shown within brackets as follows. *Amaruśataka* (A); Bhartrihari's *Nīti*, *Śringāra* and *Vairāgya Śatakatrayam* (B); *Hitopadeśa* (H); *Kirātārjunīya* of Bhāravi (K); *Mahābhārata* (M); *Panchatantra* (P); *Rāmāyana* (R); and *Siśupālavadha* of Māgha (S).

3 The opening verse of B *Śatakatrayam.*

6   Also vv. 19 and 20. See general note above for the boar
        incarnation.

7   The opening verse of *Harshacharita* by Bāṇa, court poet of
        King Harsha.

16   This commemorative verse refers to the preceding v. 15.
        Nothing is known about the person or the work named.

17   A popular description of Krishna as a little boy, from
        Krishnakarṇāmrita by Lilāshuka Bilvamangala, c. eleventh
        century.

20   The boy Krishna lifted up a hill to protect the cattle from the
        rain. See v. 24.

21   From *Bhāgavata Purāṇa*, XII. 13.2. See general note above
        for the tortoise incarnation.

31   From Nalachampu, 1.5, of Trivikrama Bhaṭṭa.

43   The verse occurs in *Kāvyamīmāmsā* of Rājaśekhara.

44   cf. note 7.

46   H, 1. 134. Vv. 47, 49, 52 are also from the same source.

48   From the poet's *Jātakamālā*, 11.18

54   B, *Nīti*. 74, with minor variation.

61   From *Śabdakalpadruma* of Udbhaṭa.

65   From *Deśopadeśa*, 1.17, of Kshemendra.

67   *Rājataringini*, 3.309.

72   B, *Nīti*. 3.

74   K, 14.24.

75   B, *Nīti*. 5.

77   P, 2.33. The sages named are well known in the history of
        Indian thought.

83   Also found with slight changes in P, 5.38; H, 1.71; and
        Chanakya Nitiśāstra, 1.69. The last line still remains a popular
        saying.

84   B, *Nīti*. 24, and H, P. 14.

90   H, 1.176.

91   *Nāgānanda*, IV. 51.

92   B, *Nīti*.72.

108   This is the thorny desert plant *Capparis aphylla*.

116   Shami is the plant *Mimosa suma* whose hardwood was
        used to kindle ritual fires.

118   The ruler Shahabuddin is dated c. 1352 CE by Peterson.

120   H, 2.19.

125   B, *Nīti*. 23.

138   Line 2 gives the literal meaning of 'khadyota', the Sanskrit
        word for firefly.

142   See note to 108.

145   P, 3.46.

152   The sandalwood tree's fragrance was traditionally supposed
        to attract snakes. Khadira is the thorny hardwood tree *Acacia
        catechu*.

156   A, 163.

163   A, 43.

165   A, 15.

166   A, 70.

169   The first two lines of the original are the same as R, Yuddha.
        5.6.

170   R, Yuddha. 5. 10 with minor variation.

171   From *Hanumannātaka* (5.25), a c. ninth-century CE play by
        Dāmodara Miśra.

172   R. Yuddha. 5.13, with minor variation.

173   *Nāgānanda*, I.

176   B, *Śringāra*. 42.

179   B, *Śringāra*. 54.

181   The poet's *Abhijnānaśākuntala*, III. 22.

182   *Chaurapanchaśikā*, 12.

183   *Abhijnānaśākuntala*, II. 10.

187   Ascribed to the poetess Mārulā in the anthology
        Sūktimuktāvali, cf. note 1 to the Introduction.

189   A, 4.

192   A, 56.

196   K, 9.43.

212   The eyes are compared to indīvara, the blue lily. Also in v. 213.

221   A, 146.

223   A, 18.

226   A, 39.

230   Ascribed to Kumāradāsa in the anthology *Śārṇgadhara Paddhati*, cf. note 1 to the Introduction. But also at A, 57.

232   A, 69.

234   *Naishadhīya-charita*, 3.163 of Harsha.

238   The poet's *Ritusamhāra* 6. 20.

242   *Ritusamhāra*, 1.13. The snake and the peacock are mortal enemies in tradition.

246   *Mrichhakaṭika* of Śūdraka, V. 16.

247   ibid. V. 14.

249   B, *Śringāra*. 92.

254   R, *Kishkindhā*. 30.58.

259   *Vikramānkadevacharita*, 16.14.

265   The poet's *Kumārasambhava*, 8.57.

266   *Ratnāvali*, III. 6.

268   *Haravijaya*, 19.5 of Ratnākara.

270   *Kumārasambhava*, 8.63.

271   An example of verse-capping. The first two lines are a statement by the lover and the rest a repartee by his inamorata. In tradition Bilhana loved a princess, and though the verse is ascribed to both, it is not found in the poet's work.

274   *Nalachampu*, 7.31.

277   A, 71. A well-known verse.

281   S, 10. 28.

285   S, 7.61.

287   *Raghuvamśa*, 16.65 of Kālidāsa.

293   *Nāgānanda*, III. 35.

295   *Kāvyālamkāra*, 7. 71.

304   K, 9.50.

309   Almost the same as A, 23.

317   Bhaṭṭikāvya (Rāvaṇavadha), 9.21

318   A, 101.

321   S. 11.

324   *Viddhaśālabhanjika*, I. 12.

325   Almost the same as A, 16.

332   Āruka is identified in Monier-William's Sanskrit–English
       dictionary as the fruit of a Himalayan plant (peach?) and Kīna
       as people in Kashmir. The turasi plant is unidentified.

338   By Rajaśekhara. Verse I. 48. It addresses the legendary
       supports of the earth and refers to Rama's feat of breaking
       Shiva's bow.

339   S, 2.46.

340   K, 11. 61.

350   *Kalāvilāsa*, 9.6, of Kshemendra.

352   *Narmamala*, 3.33, of Kshemendra.

354   *Samaya Mātrikā*, 4.23, of Kshemendra.

362   The satiric reference is to the ritual confirmation of a fee or
       gift by the donor pouring water on the hand of the recipient.

371   From the poet's *Kuṭṭanimata*, 399.

373   ibid. 822.

376   The title cited is bhaṭṭa. The possible implication is that its
       priestly bearer has twice the negative qualities of the others
       like the rustic etc. mentioned in the verse, and also frequents
       prostitutes.

377   The last item refers to the subhāshita verse, highly prized and
       sometimes plagiarized.

379   The poet's title means 'goldsmith', perhaps a professional
       indication.

389   V. 2364 also occurs in *Kalāvitasa*, 8.11, by Kshemendra.

425   See general note. The allusion is to the churning of the milky ocean, made possible by the god Vishnu, here called Krishna. Baka has over twenty citations and was perhaps the anthologist's near-contemporary. The verse refers to Sultan Zainu'l Abidin and helps to date the work.

428   This and v. 431 are taken from *Rājendrakarṇapūra*, an eulogy of the eleventh-century Kashmiri king Harshadeva by Śambhu.

436   M, *Udyoga*. 39.64.

437   M, *Śānti*. 140.23.

439   H, P.29. The thought is countered in v. 448.

446   M, Adi. 88.12.

447   H, 1.210.

448   H, P. 30.

449   M, *Śānti*. 140.24.

454   H, P. 17.

456   M, Adi. 140.82. H, 4.12.

458   M, *Śānti*. 8.19. H, 1.124.

463   *Manusmriti*, 4.119.

471   P, 4.10.

474   M, *Udyoga*. 35.56-57.

476   M, *Udyoga*. 36.30

478   P, 4.28.

485   *Prabodhachandrodaya*, II.1 of Krishna Miśra.

487   M, *Śānti*. 181.16.

491   M, *Śānti*. 331.41

502   B, *Nīti*. 84, with slight change.

505   B, *Vairāgya*. 97.

506   B, *Nīti*. 82.

508   H, 2.83.

510   P, 5.65.

515   Also quoted in *Rājataringini* of Kalhaṇa as from this author.

518   In *Rāmāyana* the hero Rama's wife was abducted while he
      had gone hunting for the golden deer.

524   Another example of statement and repartee, as in v. 271.

526   The poet's *Sevyasevakopadeśa*, v.54.

536   Ascribed to Vyāsa in *Auchitya Vichāra Charchā* of
      Kshemendra.

537   The same as *Bhagavadgītā* 2.27 except for one word.

539   H, 1.165.

540   M, Śānti. 184.15. H, 4.74.

546   *Prabodhachandrodaya*, I.29.

557   *Bhagavadgītā*, 2.61-62.

559   M, Adi. 75.50.

561   The ascription is wishful as the two poets lived at different
      times. The verse is found at B, *Śringāra*. 51.

563   B, *Śringāra*. 78, with slight change. Also ascribed in *Auchitya
      Vichāra Charchā* of Kshemendra to Chandaka.

564   B, *Vairāgya*. 12. *Vikramacharita*, J.R. 16.3. The ascription
      seems incorrect.

568   B, *Vairagya*. 7.

569   Ibid. 46.

573   Ibid. 89.

578   M, *Vana*. 117. The ascription seems incorrect.

584   Also at B, *Śringāra*. 39.

585   Also at B, *Nīti*. 45.

586   P, 1.111. H, 1.146.

The rendition of some verses sourced to H is taken from the
translator's translation of *The Hitopadeśa* of Nārāyaṇa (Penguin
India, 1998).